Taxing Subject Matters Made Easy

Learn about the tax system and how you can use the system to build wealth more efficiently if you earn income in the United States …

A Beginner's Guide to "Effective" Tax Management

TFA Financial Planning books are available at special quantity discounts for those who desire to purchase in large quantities. For more information please email: tj@thewealthincreaser.com.

Thomas (TJ) Underwood

Library of Congress Cataloging-in-Publication Data

ISBN: 978-1-953994-24-0

Publisher: TFA Financial Planning

Printed in the United States of America

Self-Published

Text design by Thomas (TJ) Underwood

Contents

Taxing Subject Matters Made Easy was created to assist you in processing tax topics and improving your thought process in other areas of your finances so that you can achieve more throughout your lifetime.

Taxing Subject Matters Made Easy

Learn about the tax system and how you can use the system to build wealth more efficiently if you earn income in the United States…

A Beginner's Guide to Effective Tax Management

Thomas (TJ) Underwood

Foreword

After several years of relatively constant market growth and relative economic certainty, the markets in the United States and worldwide took a major turn as tariffs, trade wars, economic panic and future uncertainty rocked markets worldwide.

Those occurrences collided with the ending of the 2025 tax season and the fact that I had written several books on personal finance and wealth building, yet I had not written a book on taxes.

So, I decided that the time was ripe to get this book out as soon as possible to help the millions of those who file income taxes in the United States who find the subject of taxes confusing, boring or conceptually hard to interpret utilize a better approach. It is important that you process **tax subjects** in a manner that works for you—and not against you.

In this helpful guide **"Taxing Subject Matters Made Easy"** outlines all the critical and vital knowledge and key points that all income tax filers in the United States need to know if they want to file their income taxes in a more beneficial manner as they build wealth.

I have searched back in my mind for over 30 years to ascertain "Taxing Subject Matters" that could be of most benefit to tax filers, now—and perceivably in future years.

Additionally, many thanks must go out to past and present clients as this book could not have been conceptualized and completed without their input, along with the anticipation of continually serving them and future clients.

Introduction

As a tax practitioner for over 30 years, I recently concluded that I had written numerous books, yet I had not written a book on taxes.

It then occurred to me that "now is the time" to **put a book about taxes into the marketplace** as many are suffering from anxiety about their current and future taxes—and overall finances in general in the current economy.

In this timely and to-the-point tax guide you will learn how to effectively utilize the tax knowledge that you will soon learn to achieve more at the various stages of your life.

Whether you are a novice just entering the workforce or you are one who have been paying into the tax system for years, this easy to follow guide will provide you what you need to know to make your tax management more palatable—and can further put you in position to increase your net worth and build wealth more efficiently.

Although many see taxes as being complex and boring, it does not have to be so, if it is explained and broken down in a way that you can truly understand.

That is not to say that the tax system can't get complicated, however it is to say that by learning the basics, you can put yourself in a position to understand and apply tax knowledge to your advantage and achieve goals that are near and dear to your heart on a consistent basis.

In this guide you will have the opportunity to "put yourself" in position to manage your taxes and life in a more positive, inspiring, uplifting and **results oriented** manner so that you can bring joy back into your life or rejoice in knowing that you can reach the goals that you may have thought were out of reach, so that you can ascend higher and spend more time on the beach.

This book was created as a response to the current state of economic affairs on a worldwide basis that has markets in turmoil and leadership in various areas leaving much to be desired. Despite it all, you must radiate positivity on a more consistent basis and **"Taxing Subject Matters Made Easy"** is designed to help you look within and find the strength that you need to help ensure that you succeed after this short read!

Fortunately, the unfortunate state of affairs in the spring of 2025, along with tariffs being in upheaval around the world, was used as fuel and led to the inspiration to create this book, as opposed to letting the situation take a negative turn, as the volatile market activity worldwide was unexpected and caused frustration at a certain level for many.

In life, you never know what will spark inspiration; therefore, you always want to have your antennae up for inspiration that you will receive so that you can act on that inspiration when it is in your best interest to do so—as you must always believe.

Due to the current state of affairs worldwide in the spring of 2025, you now have the opportunity to "put yourself on a path to learning more about taxes" than you ever imagined, and learn in a way that is easy on your mind, as **Taxing Subject**

Matters Made Easy, is presented in a way that is one of a kind, and in a way that allows your mind and heart to unwind as you retreat from your daily grind.

A Word About Taxes

As the blueprint for the creation of this book came into clearer focus, the 30 plus years of tax planning and preparation that I have done for numerous clients over the years also came into clearer focus.

It is my belief that those encounters during that timeline provided the insight to provide you and others a book and easily adaptable learning system. For those who file taxes in the United States and its territories around the world you can comprehend taxes in an easier to understand format. And more importantly, **Taxing Subject Matters Made Easy** can provide insight to help you and others develop the mental fortitude that is needed to implement and manage tax and financial management systems in these difficult, challenging, and uncompromising times.

It is very important that you learn and understand tax matters at a level that will allow you to succeed throughout your life—and learn a system that you truly believe in and know can work for you, as you move diligently toward making your dreams come true!

Taxing Subject Matters Made Easy is designed to inspire and show you in the easiest way possible how to manage the tax affairs in your life—even if you are not a financial professional or seasoned money manager.

It is important that you realize that taxes can get complicated, however by learning the material in this book, you will familiarize yourself with what you need to know, to ensure a more prosperous and enjoyable path toward success that you can realistically take. You can now learn in a logical, time efficient way how to manage your taxes and finances throughout your lifetime—and even after you transition. It is very important that you ask the right questions and seek the right answers on matters of significance in your life. ***Taxing Subject Matters Made Easy*** is designed to answer those questions and concerns of significance that you have and guide you on a more successful path.

By comprehending and putting into action the concepts in this book, you will become very familiar with how the tax system in the United States work and how you can use the knowledge gained to benefit yourself and your family. You can even put yourself in a position to be as much, or more prepared when it comes to taxes, as many seasoned tax professionals.

As the author of this book, and one who has spent countless hours on the creation, it is my belief that ***Taxing Subject Matters Made Easy*** *is a book that belongs in every household during these turbulent times, as your tax concerns and the management of your finances throughout your lifetime can be made much easier by reading this timely book.*

All the best to a lifetime of tax and wealth building success.

Acknowledgements

This book is the result of all the people that have been a part of my life since birth and have had a major influence on my life whether personal, business, social or any other area, as they have all played a role and helped in the creation of much of the information in this timely book.

Chapter 1 Tax Basics

Learn the importance of having a basic understanding of taxes...

It is important from a "mindset point of view" that you have a basic understanding of taxes and taxation of various sources of income.

In this chapter you will learn about areas of taxation that you need to be aware of proactively, as opposed to reactively—so that you can lighten your stress levels and achieve more.

By learning the material in this chapter early in your **life stage**, you put yourself in position to make the tax code work better for you and you make the successful building of wealth more likely to occur, right from the start.

The topics that you are about to learn in this chapter will play a large role in establishing the tax foundation that you need, so that you can put yourself in a position to succeed.

Business Taxation

If you are one who have business aspirations, be sure to choose the business structure that is the best choice from a liability and tax point of view for the type of business that you desire—and your current and long-term goals. You want to know what a **W-9 form** is and how it affects you and your business.

Be sure you are aware of the tax laws (or hire competent professionals) that affect your business—and tax plan far in advance. If you have a home-based business, you can now deduct your **home office expenses** in a less burdensome manner (simplified method in which no depreciation recapture occurs) since the passage of new regulations in 2012.

Capital Gains

If you have capital gains during the year you can offset those gains (up to $3,000) against losses—if more than $3,000 in losses, you carry the losses forward.

In 2013 the **capital gain rate** for many taxpayers, depending on their income—increased from 15% to 20%. If you have a **taxable income of $533,400 (individual) and $600,050 (joint return)** any amount over that amount would be taxed at the maximum capital gains rate of 20% (tax year 2025).

For the 2025 tax year, **individual filers** won't pay any capital gains tax if their total **taxable income** is $48,350 or less. The rate jumps to **15 percent** on capital gains, if their income is $48,351 to $533,400. Above that income level the rate climbs to **20 percent** for those who file as single.

The Filing status of **MFJ** will be taxed at 0% up to $96,700 or less. The rate jumps to 15% if their income is $96,701 to $600,050. Above that income level the rate climbs to **20 percent** for those who file.

The Filing status of **HOH** will be taxed at 0% up to $64,750 or less. The rate jumps to 15% if their income is $64,751 to $566,700.

Above that income level the rate climbs to **20 percent** for those who file.

The Filing status of **QW** will be taxed at 0% up to $96,700 and 15% over $96,701 to 600,050. Above that income level the rate climbs to **20 percent** for those who file.

Income that **exceeds the 15% maximum rates would be taxed at 20%** for each filing status. Keep in mind these numbers usually adjust upward annually.

*The capital gains rates are **0%, 15%** and **20%** and where you fall on the spectrum will be determined by your taxable income and filing status.*

Debt Cancellation

It is important that you realize that the cancellation and reduction of "certain debt" may be taxable to you.

Therefore, it is <u>your responsibility</u> to know this on the front end, prior to engaging in a debt settlement or debt reduction with any of your creditors! When a creditor cancels debt you owe, or you reach a debt settlement agreement with a creditor, the creditor would file **Form 1099-C** with the IRS if you canceled $600 or more of a debt and no exception applied (you would also receive a copy around tax filing season).

Estate Taxes

With the recent update of taxes, estate taxes receive some clarification as the first **$13.99 million** in individual estates and **$27.98 million** for family estates are now exempted from the estate tax.

Therefore, if you were the spouse and your estate was valued at $30 million, $2.02 million would be taxable based on value of your estate exceeding the exemption limit (based on the rates below), meaning you would pay over $800,000 in taxes at the federal level.

States also impose inheritance taxes as well!

The rates vary from **18% to 30%** for amounts over the federal exemption by up to **$150,000** and tops out at **40%** for estates that are more than 1 million over the federal exemption amount that is in place that adjusts annually (currently **$13.99** million).

You now have an idea of how much your heirs can expect to pay in federal estate taxes based on your estate's value after your or your loved one's transition, based on the size of the estate.

Historical Exemption Amounts

2018 $11,180,000

2019 $11,400,000

2020 $11,580,000

2021 $11,700,000

2022 $11,060,000

2023 $11,920,000

2024 $11,610,000

2025 $13,990,000

Does the estate tax expire in 2025?

If Congress doesn't act, the estate tax exemption will be sunset at the end of 2025. At that time, the exemption will drop to a base of $5 million (adjusted for inflation) in 2026. Additionally, the exemption is indexed for inflation in future years as well.

This means that, even if key TCJA provisions expire, the estate tax exemption will adjust yearly for inflation.

Most **tax-free gifts** made before the lifetime gift and estate tax exemption drops to $5 million, won't trigger higher tax bills in 2026 and beyond.

State Estate Taxes

Some states may impose an estate tax of their own (and the exemption amounts aren't always as generous as the federal estate tax exemption).

For instance, in Massachusetts, the state estate tax exemption is just $2 million and isn't indexed for inflation. In Alabama, California, Georgia and

Michigan they do not have a state estate tax. In New York, the state estate tax exemption for 2025 is $7.16 million.

In Texas, Nevada and Florida, they do not have a state estate tax. In Illinois, the state estate tax exemption is $4 million. New Jersey and Ohio estate taxes were phased out or repealed over the past decade or so.

A few states also impose an inheritance tax, which can leave a tax bill for your heirs on even small amounts of money.

Nebraska, for example, imposes an inheritance tax on adult children when their inheritance exceeds $100,000. In Kentucky, nephews and nieces only receive a $1,000 exemption.

Always factor in the state inheritance tax, as well as federal where applicable, so that you can plan better while you are alive, so that your planning can have the intended effects if you were to transition.

Excise & Other Taxes

Excise and other taxes that go by various names are also here to stay.

Whether they are called SPLOST, stormwater, fees, licensing, or the like—expect for them to increase in the future as utilities, local, state, and federal revenue must be created to fund the operations of government.

Gift Tax

The federal gift tax applies whenever you give someone besides your spouse a gift worth more than $19,000 (as of tax year 2025).

You can give up to $19,000 to as many recipients as you want without having to pay any gift tax. If you and your spouse want to gift something that you jointly own, you can **each** give up to $19,000.

If something is community property in your state, you and your spouse are each responsible for half of the value.

In all cases, you and your spouse need to ***file individual gift tax returns*** *so that you can stay in good standing with the IRS.*

When making a gift to a trust, each trust beneficiary is considered a recipient of your gift and you can still gift each beneficiary $19,000 per year as of tax year 2025.

NOTE: the **lifetime gift tax exclusion** more than doubled from 2017 to 2018 (went from 5.49 million in 2017 to 11.70 million in 2021) because of the Tax Cuts and Jobs Act, a tax reform act that passed in 2017.

As of 2025 the lifetime gift tax exclusion is **$13.99 million**, however it is expected to revert to **$5 million** in 2026 unless Congress acts.

Health Savings Accounts

What they are:

An account that is often used to pay medical expenses that occurs for an individual or family that has **major tax advantages** that include the following:

- *Contributions that are tax deductible (or contributions that are made on a pre-tax basis—if made through your employer's plan)*

- *Contributions and earnings that grow tax deferred*

- *Contributions and earnings that can be used tax free* ***for out-of-pocket medical expenses*** *in any year*

How to Qualify:

- You must have had a health insurance policy with a **deductible** of at least $1,650 individual—or $3,300 for families in 2014. And the maximum **out-of-pocket limit** is $8,300 single and $16,600 for family coverage. Additionally, individuals must not have other disqualifying medical coverage or be claimed as a dependent on someone else's tax return

- By contrast your **contribution limit** for the **2025 tax year** is $4,300 per individual and $8,550 for families (an additional $1,000 contribution is allowed if you are age 55 for the year)
- You can't make HSA contributions **after** you sign up for Medicare
- You can pay Medicare parts B and D and Medicare Advantage with your HSA account—but not Medigap
- You can pay a portion of long-term care premiums with your HSA account

How to Best Utilize:

- If you are in financial position to do so (**after you have addressed all areas of your finances appropriately**—and you have maxed out your 401k at the highest level that is allowed to get your employer match)—let your money in the HSA account grow tax-free and use it only during your elderly years or during your retirement years

- Try to pay your current year's deductibles and co-payments with your current income or savings
- Consider mutual funds and stocks (if your plan allows them in your portfolio) not just savings accounts
- Maximize your contribution—and **think long-term**—in 20 years you will be amazed at the growth of the account

Income Tax

You must look at your current income taxes that you pay at the local, state, and federal level and analyze (or pay a competent professional) them in a thorough manner to see if you can reduce or eliminate the taxes that you pay.

If you currently receive a large refund, you may want to **adjust your w-4** (payroll withholding).

Itemized Deductions

Under the "Pease Limitations" that reduce the value of itemized deductions there would be a limitation on itemized deductions.
With January 2013 legislation, the limitations were permanently repealed for many taxpayers. If you made less than $254,200 (individual) or $305,050 (joint) you would not have been affected.

For **2025**, as in 2024, 2023, 2022, 2021, 2020, 2019 and 2018, there is no limitation on itemized deductions (referred to as the "Pease" limitation under prior law), because that limitation was also suspended by the **TCJA** for years 2018-2025.

Mortgage Debt Relief Act

If you find yourself in the position where you may have to sell your home because of a "Short Sale" or you faced or are facing foreclosure or you had a loan modification that did not work out, you still have relief as the **Mortgage Debt Relief Act of 2007** was extended to **January 1st of 2014** and then "extended yet again" until tax year **2025**. The extension means that if you faced a short sale, foreclosure or loan modification—you would possibly be excluded from paying taxes on the debt that was forgiven.

The **Mortgage Insurance Premium Deduction** for homeowners and tax filers who put less than 20% down **was extended for tax year 2013—2021**, meaning that in addition to your interest, property tax and possibly points—you could continue deducting the portion of your housing payment that goes toward the payment of the insurance premium.

Whether the premium was for an FHA **(MIP)** or Conventional loan **(PMI),** the insurance premium was deductible during those years. The deduction expired at the end of 2021, so this insurance **isn't tax deductible** for **tax year 2022 and beyond tax returns**, unless Congress acts.

Payroll Taxes (Social Security, Medicare & other Withholdings)

Although your Social Security and Medicare withholdings are mandated by law, **you may be able to control** other areas of your withholdings.

You control your w-4 withholding—your retirement contributions (if you have an employer who provides a match it may be wise to contribute at a level of the match at a minimum), HSA/FSA—and other withholdings that you qualify for and your employer may offer.

Be sure to consider an IRA if you qualify—**Traditional or Roth**. A **traditional** has the potential to reduce your yearly taxes and help you save for your future—you would be taxed at withdrawal.

A **ROTH** provides no immediate tax reduction—but your **contributions and earnings would grow tax free,** and you can withdraw your **"contributions"** tax-free at basically any time.

Property Taxes

You must analyze your current property taxes and if you feel they are too high you can utilize the appeal process to possibly get them reduced! Be sure that you know the property tax amount that you currently pay and be sure that you have properly applied for the homestead exemption and other exemptions that may be available in your community.

You also want to know the strength or weakness of your local government as they possess the power to increase or decrease your future Millage Rates. By knowing the condition of your government, you can better plan for the likelihood of tax increases in the future.

You can possibly find the tax rate in your community or a community that you plan on moving to by searching public sites on the web. On many of the sites you will have to click on "calculators" and then "data tools" to get the rates needed. Your real estate agent can also provide you with this information.

Also be aware of stormwater fees, special assessments, excise fees, emergency fees, garbage fees, **sp**ecial **l**ocal **o**ption **s**ales **t**axes etcetera, that are in effect "taxes by another name" as they are increasing in popularity in many states and localities.

You can also go to retirementliving.com to get an overview of property and other taxes in your state—or a state that you anticipate moving to.

Always realize that "property taxes" are local in nature, which means they can vary significantly from state to state, county to county—or city to city!

Rental

If you have rental properties, you can utilize them to possibly decrease your annual taxes if you file them on **schedule E** (Rental Property form) or a **K-1 partnership** tax return.

If you have the property set up under a **schedule C**—self-employed form, you can also possibly utilize the rental properties on your personal tax return to help reduce your taxes owed or increase your refund amount.

Rental property deductions and the proper use of depreciation are a few of the major deductions left for the modest income taxpayer.

Rental property owners who have a **modified adjusted gross income** of $100,000 or less are permitted by the IRS to deduct up to $25,000 in rental real estate losses each year that the property is in service (they actively participate in rental activity). Phaseouts occur, and when those with a **m**odified **a**djusted **g**ross **i**ncome of more than $150,000, aren't extended the allowance at all.

However, the same rules **don't apply to real estate** professionals. Rental property owners who are real estate professionals in the eyes of the IRS **are allowed to deduct any amount of losses** from their other non-passive income.
If your rental properties are **"corporately held"** you would possibly gain a tax advantage on your corporation's return.

If you had a **pass-through corporation** (S-corporation) you would possibly have "taxable income" on your personal tax return. If the S corporation reported a loss—you could possibly reduce the amount of taxes that you owe or increase your refund amount on your personal tax return.

Retirement

It is important that you have a realistic understanding of how your retirement income will be taxed at the state as well as federal level!

You must have a basic understanding (right now) of how your Estate & Inheritance taxes, Social Security Benefits, IRA's, Pensions & Other Retirement Accounts, will be taxed during your retirement years.

The taxation of retirement income is consistent at the federal level—but varies greatly from state to state. Be sure you understand the taxation of your retirement income in your state!

Do you know if estate and/or inheritance taxes are applicable in your state based on the size and value of your estate?

Do you know if Social Security benefits will be taxed in your state or the state that you plan on retiring in?

Do you know the States that don't tax income at all (Alaska, Florida, Nevada, South Dakota, Texas, Washington and Wyoming)?

Do you know if there are exclusions in your state that allow some or all your retirement income to be excluded from taxation?

For example—in the State of Georgia there is a generous **retirement income exclusion** of $65,000 for taxpayers 65 and older ($130,000 if Married Filing Jointly). Those ages 62 to 64 can take a $35,000 exemption per person as of tax year 2025.

Did you know that **6 States** (California, Minnesota, Nebraska, North Dakota, Rhode Island and Vermont) **offer no exclusions at all** for retirement income?

In short, it is <u>your responsibility</u> to look into how your taxes will be affected during your retirement years at both the federal **and** state level!

Sale of Residence

The sale of your residence if done properly could lead to a real windfall for you and your family.
If you remain at the residence for **2 plus years** and later sell your property at a gain—you can exclude $250,000 of the gain if you are single and up to $500,000 of the gain if you are married.
Be sure you know all of the parameters involved if you are considering selling your home and you want to exclude the gain from taxation.

Note: if a portion of your residence is used for business and depreciation is deducted on your taxes in the traditional manner, that portion will be subject to recapture (will be taxed at time of sale)—thus the amount of your excluded gain will possibly be reduced.

Sales Tax

Sales tax vary from state to state in the United States. Some states tax food at a lower rate or not at all, and some states do not have sales tax at all.

Other goods and services are taxed at varied rates based on the laws of a particular state or locality.

You must realize that sales taxes are here to stay, and you must be prepared to pay them now and in the future.

Unless you live in Alaska, Delaware, Montana, New Hampshire, or Oregon you will have to pay sales tax on your purchases.

If you travel a lot, be sure that you understand that hotel and lodging taxes vary substantially from state to state and even city to city—in the same state.

Lodging taxes are levied by your state or local government and can go by different names, including sales tax, transient tax, hotel tax, room tax, occupation tax, and many more. Guests are required to pay these taxes on top of the cost of their accommodation.

You may pay as low as 9.4% in Colorado Springs, Colorado to as high as 17.5% in Birmingham, Alabama. The average rate usually fluctuates in the 13% to 14% range—across the United States, however changes of an upward nature are not uncommon.

To find the sales tax rate in your state—or a state that you plan on moving to or visit, go to the "States" tax page.

Additionally, bed and breakfast, Air B-n-B and other "new economy" accommodations will also normally have a tax structure at the local and state level, so if you visit those environments, be prepared to pay a tax.

Social Security

You can determine if your Social Security benefits are taxable by calculating your combined income. This includes your adjusted gross income (AGI), half of your annual Social Security benefits, and any tax-exempt interest (like income from municipal bonds).

If this total goes over the IRS threshold, part of your benefits will feature into your taxable income. However, it's important to realize that this rule only applies to Social Security benefits—meaning Supplemental Security Income (SSI) benefits are not taxable. SSI is a separate program designed to help low-income seniors and people with disabilities cover basic needs like food, housing, and clothing. It's also worth researching how your individual state handles Social Security taxes.

If you're single and your combined income is between $25,000 and $34,000, up to 50% of your Social Security benefits could be taxable. If that number goes over $34,000, up to 85% of your benefits can be taxed. For married couples filing jointly, the limits are a bit higher—up to 50% of your benefits could be taxed if your combined income exceeds $32,000, and up to 85% can be taxed if your income exceeds $44,000.

Say a retiree gets $20,000 in Social Security benefits and earns another $15,000 from a part-time job. The IRS would calculate their income by adding half of their Social Security benefits ($10,000) to their other income ($15,000). That brings their total to $25,000. Since this is right at the lower threshold for single filers, up to 50% of their Social Security benefits could be taxed.

For a married couple with a combined income of $75,000 that also receives $40,000 in benefits, their taxable portion is much higher. The IRS adds half of their Social Security benefits ($20,000) to their other income ($75,000), bringing their total to $95,000, well above the highest threshold. That means up to 85% of their Social Security benefits could be taxed.

How you file your taxes matters, too. If you are married, do you file jointly or separately? Should you file as MFS? Maybe, maybe not. Filing separately might reduce how much of your Social Security benefits are taxed, but it can come with trade-offs. Couples who file separately lose access to certain tax deductions and credits, and they also face lower IRA contribution limits. That's why it's worth talking to a tax professional who can help figure out which filing status might work best for your specific situation.

It's also worth mentioning that your investment choices can affect how much of your Social Security benefits get taxed. For example, municipal bonds are usually tax-free at the federal level, but they aren't always exempt from state or local taxes. That means they might still count toward your combined income, which could push more of your Social Security benefits into the taxable range.

Stepped-Up Basis

It is important that you understand the concept of **"stepped-up basis"** as it simply means that you will get a break on your taxes if you inherit a house, stocks, bonds, mutual funds etcetera from your parent(s) or spouse **due to the value being assessed at the current market price**, not the value when it was purchased.

If your parent(s) were to transition and as part of the estate, you received a house currently valued at $350,000—but the property was purchased by your parent(s) 30 years ago for $50,000, you would not owe taxes on $300,000 (the difference between purchase price and the current value if you were to sell immediately after your parents transition).

Instead, if you sold the property for $350,000, **you would owe zero** in taxes.

If you sold the property for $400,000, **you would owe taxes on $50,000** ($400,000 minus $350,000)—meaning the value of the property was "stepped-up" to the current market value of $350,000.

That is important information to know on the front end whether you are inheriting property or plan on leaving property for your heirs!

It is important to realize that in similar fashion stocks, bonds and mutual funds also receive **"stepped up basis"** treatment when they are inherited.

If your parents purchased stocks 20 years ago for $15,000 and at the time of their transition the stocks are worth $200,000, **your basis would be "stepped-up" to $200,000** and if you sold the stocks immediately for $200,000, you would owe zero in taxes.

If you sold the stocks 2 years later for $300,000, **you would owe taxes on $100,000** ($300,000 minus $200,000) instead of $285,000 ($300,000 minus the $15,000 original cost or basis).

Always realize that inherited IRA's whether ROTH or Traditional can be tricky—as there are certain rules, guidelines and nuances that must be adhered to if your goal is to minimize your taxes.

Be sure to utilize competent professionals if you were to inherit a home, stocks, bonds, mutual funds etcetera—whether inside or outside of a retirement account.

In addition, be aware that if your parents **had income** (salary, interest, dividends etcetera) **that was owed to them at the time of their transition**—income tax could still be owed on the income, and you might be **required** to pay it.

NOTE: Always keep the federal and state exemption amounts in mind when you are receiving or leaving property because of a loved one's transition—or your transition.

Even though you may be eligible for the federal exemption if your estate is smaller than 13.99 million (2025 limit) and possibly double that amount if it was your spouse who transitioned, you may indeed owe at the state level, so always keep that in mind when doing your tax planning.

Tariffs

A tariff is a tax imposed by one country on the goods and services imported from another country to influence it, raise revenues, or protect competitive advantages. And even though it is not a direct tax to you, you would feel the impact of a tariff in the form of higher prices. Most countries are limited by their natural resources and ability to produce certain goods and services.

Countries trade with other countries to get what their population needs and demands by tampering with the tariff rate(s) and if done strategically it could be effective in a number of areas!

If done haphazardly, imposing tariffs can cause more problems than it solves. The effects of tariffs on most taxpayers are regressive in nature, meaning those who earn the least are affected the most.

By contrast, income taxes are progressive in nature, meaning those who earn more are taxed at a higher rate and theoretically pay more in taxes, however loopholes often allow many to avoid taxation on large amounts of income.

Tax Preparation

For income tax preparation you can utilize the tax professional of your choice, including attorneys and CPAs.

Or if your tax situation is not very complicated you can choose among tax software companies or other reputable companies who provide tax services.

Tax History in the United States

To pay for the **War of 1812** (conflict between the United States and the British Empire from 1812 to 1815), Congress passed new internal taxes on refined sugar, carriages, distillers and auction sales and reinstated the Commissioner of the Revenue to collect them. On August 24, 1814, the British burned the Treasury building in Washington, D.C.

On December 23, 1817, Congress repealed these and all remaining internal taxes and abolished the position of the Commissioner of the Revenue and all offices to collect them.

The **taxation of income** in the United States, according to many, began during the civil war but was suspended after the war.

In 1913, the income tax returned and since that time it has been here to stay!

The need to finance the Civil War created **one of the first versions** of a "federal income tax" in 1862. The U.S. income tax was officially born on February 3, 1913, when Congress ratified the **16th amendment** to the U.S. Constitution.

Less than 1% of Americans had to pay the tax in its earliest days.

Since that time, major tax reforms have been ongoing for decades:

- The federal income tax as we know it was officially born on February 3, 1913, when Congress ratified the 16th Amendment to the U.S. Constitution after an on-again-off-again start that lasted decades.

- The amendment read, "Congress shall have the power to lay and collect taxes on incomes, from whatever source derived, without apportionment among the several states, and regard to any census or enumeration."

- However, less than 1% of Americans had to pay the tax in the first days after its inception, thanks to the amendment's provisions for numerous taxpayer-friendly deductions and exemptions. The rate was only 1% of net income at that point.

- Congress later added a 6% rate for incomes of more than $500,000.

- Numerous tweaks and add-ons occurred in the 1940s. The Revenue Act of 1942 increased tax rates and the number of citizens who had to pay it.

- The Current Tax Payment Act passed in 1943, heralding the beginning of the **tax withholding process** by employers.

- **The top individual marginal income tax rate tended to increase over time** through the early 1960s, with some additional bumps during war years.

- The **top income tax rate reached above 90%** from 1944 through 1963, peaking in 1944, when top taxpayers **paid an income tax rate of 94%** on their taxable income.

- Standard deductions were created in 1944 with the passage of the Individual Income Tax Act.

- "The withholding system **(implemented in 1943)** was implemented simply because the collection was easy, according to many at the time—and not because it was the soundest, most equitable, or most efficient tax system.

- However, the Internal Revenue Service attempted to make the tax process more efficient over the years. The first toll-free telephone line was introduced in 1965. Electronic filing began in 1986, although it was limited at first. Taxpayers who owed money were able to electronically file their returns beginning in 1992.

- Currently the IRS offers electronic filing, rapid refund options, electronic payment of income taxes, electronic payment of estimated taxes and many other new technology perks.

Source: Internal Revenue Service. "Historical Highlights of the IRS."

- **The Alternative Minimum Tax (AMT)**

The AMT was created in **1969** because it was found that a few hundred high-income individuals were able to use a combination of exclusions, deductions, and credits to pay little or no income tax.

- **The Tax Reform Act (TRA)**

The Tax Reform Act that was launched in **1986** under then president Ronald Reagan shook up the tax system yet again as it broadened the AMT so more high-income individuals would be subject to it.

"The Tax Reform Act of 1986 made numerous changes to the tax law including **taxing ordinary and capital gains income at the same rate and there were only two brackets** (15% and 28%).

It also added **passive activity loss limitation rules** that shut down a tax shelter industry that many middle-to high-income individuals had been using to minimize their taxes.

- **The American Taxpayer Relief Act (ATRA)**

The American Taxpayer Relief Act (ATRA) restored the top income tax rate to 39.6% in **2012** after it was cut to 35% by President George W. Bush's tax cuts in 2001 and 2003. The **American Taxpayer Relief Act of 2012** (**ATRA**) was enacted and passed by the United States Congress on January 1, 2013, and was signed into law by U.S. President Barack Obama the next day.

- **The Tax Cuts & Jobs Act of 2017**

The Tax Cuts and Jobs Act of 2017 (TCJA) is the unofficial name for the large set of changes to the

Revenue Code of 1986, signed into law by President Trump in 2017. TCJA made many large changes across multiple areas of the tax code, including **most infamously reducing the corporate tax rate, increasing the standard deduction, and increasing the <u>applicable exclusion amounts</u> for estate taxes,** all of which you are probably aware of.

Only some of the TCJA changes were permanent, and over twenty provisions will expire by the end of 2025. Notable tax changes from the act include the following:

1) Reduced the seven brackets from 10%, 15%, 25%, 28%, 33%, 35%, and 39.6% respectively to 10%, 12%, 22%, 24%, 32%, 35%, and 37%. The income levels for the brackets were slightly increased, which generally reduced taxes for many individuals.
2) The TCJA greatly increased the standard deduction from $6,500 to $12,000 for

individuals and from $13,000 to $24,000 for those filing jointly. This increase in standard deduction **greatly reduced** the number of individuals who benefit from itemizing deductions.

3) The deduction for interest on home mortgages and equity was altered to reduce the **mortgage limit to $750,000** and to limit eligible home equity.
4) State and local tax **(SALT)** deductions became **capped** at $10,000.
5) Miscellaneous tax deductions for things like **workplace expenses for employees** were "completely" eliminated. All these changes will revert to their pre-TCJA provisions after 2025.

- **The Inflation Reduction Act (IRA) came along in 2022**. The Inflation Reduction Act included numerous new and modified energy credits for individuals and businesses. It's possible that some of these credits may be repealed or downsized as part of any extension of expiring provisions of the TCJA.

Excise and "Sin" Taxes

Taxation doesn't begin and end with those imposed on income and earnings. Excise taxes, often called "sin" taxes, can take a hefty bite out of taxpayers' pocket and bank accounts as well. These taxes are imposed on the sale of specific products and services.

The ***first major excise tax*** *in the United States was on whiskey in* ***1791****, sparking the Whiskey Rebellion, but the tax was later repealed.*

Over time, states began implementing sin taxes on tobacco, alcohol, and gambling, with the primary goal shifting towards public health and deterring unhealthy behaviors.

Excise taxes are generally paid by retailers, producers, and wholesalers, but these entities will often pass them down to you, if you engage in any so called "sin" activities. The excise tax on cigarettes averages about $1 a pack. Beer and wine are typically taxed at a lower rate than distilled spirits.

Commonly affected purchases subject to excise taxes include alcohol, tobacco, health insurance, and gasoline.

“The key purpose of “**excise taxes”** on alcohol and tobacco are to tax undesired behavior, particularly the purchase of cigarettes by young people, and to generate a small amount of revenue.

There are several federal excise taxes, but the ones on alcohol, tobacco, and gasoline are best known.

Excise taxes are a small part of government tax collections, representing less than 2% of total federal tax revenues.

Excise taxes on alcohol and tobacco traditionally lead to increased prices at the time of the retail sale.

This price increase is designed to reduce consumption which can have the follow-along effect of a decrease in consumption that can lead to reducing health issues.

Many consumers continue to spend that extra dollar on a pack of cigarettes, but it's a good bet that their wallets will feel the effect because they must additionally deal with income tax on money they earn throughout the year.

Conclusion or Key Points

Taxation in the U.S. has always been frowned upon by those who must pay, and this attitude has been exacerbated by all its various applications from the filing of income taxes where those who make the most seem to pay the least percentage wise, to the payment of taxes on real property, to that modest purchase you just made at your favorite store this week.

Your awareness of "tax basics" **that you have learned in this chapter, along with the history of the tax system in the United States**, has given you a strong foundation on which to build your tax knowledge that you will soon learn throughout the rest of this book.

Always realize that small changes in taxation occur annually! In many cases, just when you get familiar with the prior year's changes, new changes are imposed!

Although tax changes are inevitable, so too should your attitude toward adjusting positively to those changes be inevitable. As an informed taxpayer you can benefit from keeping a watchful eye on the ever-evolving changes and checking in with your tax professional(s) when tax changes are made so they can best prepare you for the impact, whether those changes are for your benefit—or detriment—prior to the filing of your current (or prior) year's taxes.

Chapter 2 Employee Withholdings

Learn more at this time about W-4 and other withholdings and how you can maximize your tax position...

As the new year and tax season comes in annually, many have questions or concerns about their federal (and state) tax withholdings by their employer, and they want to know how they can more effectively manage those withholdings.

In this chapter you will learn in detail how "withholdings on income" earned in the United States occur, so that you or those whom you know can utilize the system to achieve more.

W-4 Employee's Withholding Certificate

Your employer provides you withholding for income tax purposes upon hire, or upon request if you are a current employee. That opportunity could allow you the chance to adjust withholding amounts by changing certain elections and/or having additional amounts withheld.

By adjusting your withholding amounts, you can get to a point where you have a designated amount withheld so that you can get a refund or owe—or increase/decrease the amount of the refund or increase/decrease the amount that you will owe the IRS. Your withholding for the year would be displayed on your form W-2 that you get at tax time from your employer (usually in January or February).

Before 2020, you had to claim a certain number of withholding allowances on **form W-4** (you could also pick zero). The amount of federal income tax withheld from your paycheck was then based on how many allowances you claimed. The more allowances that you claimed, the less the IRS would withhold. Prior to the change you could claim fewer allowances than what you were entitled to if you wanted to increase your withholding, but you couldn't claim more allowances.

Allowances are no longer allowed on the new form that went into effect in 2020!

Generally, upon hire you would complete **Form W-4** so that your employer could withhold the correct federal income tax from your pay based on what you desire. If changes are needed, you can complete a new **form W-4** each year and particularly when your personal or financial situation changes. Depending on the size of your employer, the process would be done through your Human Resources or Payroll department—or if a small operation, is conducted by your manager or other designated individual(s).

Key factors since the arrival of the new form now include:

Step 1: personal information (name, address, SSN) and Single, MFJ, or HOH election

Step 2: multiple jobs or spouse works election

Step 3: the number of qualifying children under age 17 multiplied by $2,000 and the number of dependents multiplied by $500 can be entered based on the amount calculated—and if you plan on being eligible for other credits, that estimated amount can also be entered into the calculation

Step 4: other income, deductions and extra withholdings **(key step for adjustment from your current withholding)**, and additionally if you expect to have other income such as interest, dividends, retirement income and/or you expect to itemize—you can include extra withholdings based on your own situation

Step 5: you would sign and date

The IRS (IRS.gov) now offers **a tax estimator** that many find helpful when deciding on their withholding amounts.

Estimated Taxes

If you are self-employed or have W-2 income you can elect to pay estimated taxes and if you choose this option, payments are expected to be paid to the IRS based on your income at intervals of **April 15, June 15, September 15 and January 15** of the new year through the EFTPS (you set up online and in a week or so you will receive correspondence in the mail that allows you to finalize setup and start making payments electronically) system or other arrangement that you can set up with the IRS that would allow you to make timely payments.

Once your account is set up securely through the ***EFTPS*** *system you can make payment for the current interval and also schedule payments for up to 3 additional intervals based on the payment date(s) that you select (be sure your account is adequately funded on the dates that you elect to pay), thereby ensuring that you avoid underpayment penalties if your estimate of taxes you owe is accurate or fairly accurate.*

Individuals, including sole proprietors, partners, and S corporation shareholders, generally have to make estimated tax payments if they expect to owe tax of $1,000 or more when their return is filed.

Corporations generally must make estimated tax payments if they expect to owe tax of $500 or more when their return is filed.

You may have to pay estimated tax for the current year if your tax was more than zero in the prior year.

See the worksheet in **Form 1040-ES, Estimated Tax for Individuals** for more details on who must pay estimated tax.

You don't have to pay estimated tax for the current year if you meet all three of the following conditions.

- **You had no tax liability for the prior year**

- **You were a U.S. citizen or resident alien for the whole year**

- **Your prior tax year covered a 12-month period**

You had no tax liability for the prior year if your total tax was zero or you didn't have to file an income tax return!

For additional information on how to figure your estimated tax, refer to Publication 505, Tax Withholding and Estimated Tax.

To figure your estimated tax, you must figure your expected adjusted gross income, taxable income, taxes, deductions, and credits for the year.

Estimated tax payments are generally due:

- **April 15** for income earned January 1 to March 31 **(months 1, 2 and 3 of year)**

- **June 15** for income earned April 1 to May 31 **(months 4 and 5 of year)**

- **September 15** for income earned June 1 to August 31 **(months 6, 7, and 8 of year)**

- **January 15** of the following year for income earned September 1 to December 31 **(months 9 through 12 of year)**

https://www.irs.gov/payments/pay-as-you-go-so-you-wont-owe-a-guide-to-withholding-estimated-taxes-and-ways-to-avoid-the-estimated-tax-penalty.

Interest

Non-corporate overpayment 8%

Corporate overpayment 7%

Underpayment corporate/non-corporate 8%

Note: Interest rates may change from year-to-year, the interest categories listed above are for tax year 2024 and the rates may change in future years.

It is also important to distinguish whether you are an employee (employer can withhold taxes) or an independent contractor (you are responsible for paying taxes) so that you can stay in good standing with the IRS.

W-9 and Business Transactions

If you are a business owner, you may want those who you do business with to submit a **W-9 form** so that you can withhold taxes or report withholding or payments made to them based on their business identification number, social security number or **T**axpayer **I**dentification **N**umber if a sole proprietor.

You too can use Form W-9 to provide your correct Taxpayer Identification Number (TIN) to the person or business who is required to file an information return with the IRS to report, for example:

- **Income is paid to you.**
- **Real estate transactions.**
- **Mortgage interest you paid.**
- **Acquisition or abandonment of secured property.**
- **Cancellation of debt.**
- **Contributions you made to an IRA.**
- **Gambling winnings.**

Learn more by going to the IRS website at IRS.gov...

FICA

The **F**ederal **I**nsurance **C**ontributions **A**ct **of 1935 (FICA)** was signed into law to allow money to be withheld to help establish and keep the Social Security system solvent and ensure that current recipients receive their payments.

On your paycheck or pay stub, you will see **Social Security withholdings (6.2%)** up to a wage limit which "adjusts annually" and **Medicare withholding (1.45%)** "which is unlimited" under current law.

The current total tax rate for Social Security is 6.2% for the employer and 6.2% for the employee, or **12.4%** total.

The current rate for Medicare is 1.45% for the employer and 1.45% for the employee, or **2.9%** total.

The combined rate for Social Security and Medicare employer and employee rate is 15.3% total.

There's a maximum <u>wage base</u> for Social Security taxes on earnings, above which no tax is levied.

The wage base is set at $168,600 for 2024, and for earnings in 2025, the base or "taxable maximum" is <u>$176,100</u>. Always keep in mind, the wage base adjusts annually.

Again, keep in mind there is **no wage base limit** for Medicare taxes.

Other

<u>HSA/FSA</u> and <u>retirement accounts</u> are often withheld by employees who elect the withholding and it is usually a wise choice, as that allows for the" lowering of taxes" since it is done on a pre-tax basis, therefore it does not go into your taxable income calculation and can lead to a substantial financial windfall for you and your family if utilized effectively.

<u>Social Security income</u> does not require withholding; however, you have the option of having taxes withheld if you desire. Medicare payments can also be withheld from your monthly Social Security payments if you find it convenient to do so and you choose Medicare for health coverage at age 65.

If you received Social Security income you would receive a **<u>1099-SSA form</u>** during the tax season and you would include that income along with your other income to determine how much would be taxable up to a maximum of 85%.

If you had taxes or Medicare premiums withheld, they would be displayed on form 1099-SSA.

Pension income you can generally elect to have withholdings from pension provider by making the election and completing form W-4p which is very similar to the W-4 process mentioned earlier in this discussion.

Self-employment income does not require withholding, but estimated taxes are expected to be paid to the IRS based on your income at intervals of **April 15, June 15, September 15 and January 15** of the new year, so if you are self-employed (or an independent contractor) be aware of your responsibilities.

You can deduct ordinary and necessary expenses from your self-employment earnings to help reduce the amount that will be taxable.

Among others, the deductions include advertising, commissions, postage, phone, utilities, supplies, medical coverage, office expenses, automobile, equipment, furniture and any other expenses related to your business that qualify according to IRS guidelines, and those expenses can be deducted from your income to help reduce the taxes that you will owe at tax time, thereby "lowering your estimated tax payments" that are due on the dates mentioned above.

You can also use retirement plans, including SEP-IRAs (up to 25% of earnings can be contributed) to further reduce the amount that would be subject to taxation. Self-employment earnings of $400 or more would also be subject to SE taxation and you would also be able to deduct 1/2 of your SE tax payment on your personal 1040 return. Your earnings and deductions from self-employment as a sole proprietor would go on **schedule C** and be carried over to **schedule 1** and then **1040** page 1.

Your earnings that you pay taxes on through self-employment would be used in the 35-year average that is used to calculate your social security benefits when you retire (generally age 62 to age 70), so be aware of that factor.

Qualified Business Income may offer you the opportunity to pay less in taxes if you qualify and you timely file your tax return.

Gaming/gambling winnings may have tax withholds up to 24% at the federal level. Be sure to keep good records as **winnings can be offset against losses** to help reduce your taxes. With certain gambling winnings you would receive a form **W-2G** during the tax season for winnings you had in the previous year.

Unemployment Compensation you could choose to have taxes withheld or you can choose not to. Unemployment compensation requires payment of taxes, so be sure to plan for the payment at the federal and possibly state level. If you receive unemployment compensation you will receive a **1099-G** during the tax season the year after you receive compensation.

IRAs and retirement accounts may be subject to withholding unless an exception applies. Early withdrawals could also result in an additional penalty. If contributions are made through payroll, they could possibly avoid taxation and penalty until withdrawal at retirement time if you did not tap into the account(s) early. Your retirement income would generally be reported to you on form 1099R which is similar in content to that of a form W-2 mentioned earlier, your withholdings would be done through a form W-4p which is similar in scope to that of a W-4 that was mentioned earlier. Your traditional IRA and Retirement accounts would generally be taxed at your ordinary income tax rate.

Form 1098 although "no withholding" is done on form **1098 Mortgage Interest Statement**, it is included in this chapter due to the importance that it plays in the building of wealth. You would receive **form 1098** at tax time if you are a homeowner and it provides in documented form your outstanding mortgage loan balance (usually balance at beginning of tax year) mortgage points paid if any, principal, and interest paid for the year—along with private mortgage insurance or MIP for **those who put less than 20% down** at the time of their home purchase.

Escrow payments made for property taxes may also be included. The mortgage interest along with property taxes paid can be deducted on schedule A for those who itemize, and mortgage interest, property taxes along with other deductions, can play an important role in reducing taxes or increasing the refund amount that you would receive. By **strategically planning** in advance, you can plan from year to year and that planning can play an important role in helping you build wealth more efficiently.

1099-K income is income that is often earned in the new gig economy, and **"Taxing Subjects Made Easy"** would be remiss not to include this income in this chapter, as 1099k income is subject to taxation and no withholding for tax purposes are done, therefore it is the responsibility of the recipient of 1099-K income to report the income and pay taxes on that income.

Keep in mind the IRS receives a copy of this and virtually all other forms of income that has been discussed in this chapter.

Whether you resell clothing, household items or other goods or **perform** services and an electronic record is kept—you may have to report that income, depending on the amount. This includes Air B-N-B, VRBO, Uber, lift, Grubhub and a vast array of delivery services and rideshare income that are derived over electronic platforms.

Although there was a back and forth on reporting **1099-K** income for several years, the form is now active and online marketplace or third-party apps must report when certain thresholds are met (generally when goods and/or services total over $5,000 for tax year 2024 but scheduled to begin at $600 in the future), therefore if you are part of the gig economy, you want to plan now for the payment of taxes.

Other sources of income depending on type may also be subject to withholding. Also be aware of taxation at the state and local levels as it is important to look at your taxes in a comprehensive or wholesome way and analyze from <u>ALL sources</u>—even when what are really taxes, go by other names.

In addition, liens, child support and garnishment of your pay can occur (involuntary withholdings) and that is the type of withholding you want to avoid as best you can.

Filing Penalties

1. Your failure to pay (**ftp**) in a timely manner could lead to a "tax penalty" for underpayment of your federal taxes. The failure to pay penalty is 0.5% of the unpaid taxes for each month or part of a month the tax remains unpaid. The penalty won't exceed 25% of your unpaid taxes.
2. The failure to file (**ftf**) penalty applies if you don't file your tax return by the due date (including extensions).

The IRS calculates failure to file penalty in this way:

- Tax required to be shown on the return,
- Less tax paid on time (example: withholding credits or estimated tax payments),
- Less available refundable credits, then
- Multiplied by 5% per month (up to 25%).
- If the return is more than 60 days late, the minimum penalty is the amount listed or 100% of the underpayment, whichever is less.
- If both failure to pay and failure to file apply—an offset is available

3. The **Failure to Deposit** Penalty applies to employers that don't make employment tax deposits. If you are an employer and have employees, you want to avoid the failure to deposit (**ftd**) penalty(s) which are imposed if you fail to pay:

- On time
- In the right amount
- In the right way

Employer-paid taxes include federal income tax, Social Security and Medicare taxes and Federal Unemployment Tax. Employers must send employment tax deposits to the IRS on a monthly or semi-weekly schedule.

The penalty you pay is a percentage of the taxes you did not deposit on time, in the right amount or in the right way, the IRS calculates the Failure to Deposit Penalty based on the number of calendar days your deposit is late, starting from its due date. The normal penalty range is from 2% to 10%, depending on how late the deposit is.

4. **The "failure to file" form 1065** was part of the legislative mandate in Section 1224 of the Taxpayer Relief Act of 1997 that requires partnerships with more than 100 partners to file their return on magnetic media (electronically as prescribed by the IRS Commissioner)

for taxable years ending after December 31, 2000. For returns required to be filed after December 31, 2015, a penalty of $260 for each Schedule K-1 over 100 will be assessed.

If the partnership feels they can establish reasonable cause due to hardship after the penalty is assessed, they may request abatement of the penalty in writing. If the partnership feels that reasonable cause should be considered in relation to their penalty assessment, they should not wait for the penalty to be assessed to request such an abatement.

Reasonable Cause Penalty Abatement

With all IRS penalties mentioned above, there is a possible out.

Reasonable causes are determined on a case-by-case basis considering all the facts and circumstances of your situation.

Reasons that qualify for relief due to reasonable cause depend on the type of penalty you owe and the laws in the Internal Revenue Code (IRC) for each penalty.

Examples of valid reasons for failing to file or pay on time may include:

- **Fires, natural disasters or civil disturbances**
- **Inability to get records**
- **Death, serious illness or unavoidable absence of the taxpayer or immediate family member**
- **System issues that delayed a timely electronic filing or payment**

Conclusion or Key Points

It is important that you realize that taxation of income at this time in the United States appears here to stay, and if you have income you want to come up with a way to pay your taxes "as you earn" whether by **w-4 withholdings** through your **"payroll withholdings"** as you earn or through the payment of **"estimated taxes"** based on what you earn throughout the year and pay at designated intervals in April, June, September and January.

By timely managing your finances and paying your taxes you can avoid large tax payments and penalties at tax time that could severely hamper your wealth building efforts.

Although you are the ultimate decision maker, a refund of $1,000 or owing $1,000 to the IRS is a reasonable target to aim for, assuming your finances are in order from a comprehensive perspective, and you have a **strong money management** personality.

By "planning in advance" you can manage your finances and taxes in a manner where you owe a little—or get a little back, thereby minimizing the financial stress in your life, preventing large losses due to fraud, investing what you would otherwise allow the IRS to hold and otherwise manage your finances more optimally.

Also, don't forget about the taxation of your assets upon sale, as in many cases you will be taxed at your ordinary income or the generally more favorable capital gains rate!

Your withholdings along with your standard deduction or itemized deduction amount, and other **adjustments deductions and credits** will play a large role in determining if you will owe or if you will get a refund in this and the coming tax seasons.

Always realize that "even if you don't have any income tax withheld" from your wages, you may get a refund if you are eligible for tax credits such as the Earned Income Credit, the Additional Child Tax Credit, American Opportunity Credit and other potential credits that you may qualify for.

Therefore, you would want to ensure that you file your taxes in a timely manner (you have a 3-year window to file—including extensions, otherwise you lose the refund) as that can put you in better position to manage your money at the various stages of your life.

Also, you can elect to file for an extension to pay your taxes **(up to October 15th)** if you find yourself in the unfortunate position of not planning or planning inappropriately due to lack of knowledge, life stress, or not knowing about the payment of taxes to the degree that you now know!

You and your tax practitioner can extend the deadline for months (by filing form 4868) to give you additional time to come up with the funds needed to pay your taxes.

However, payment is required (or at least suggested) based on what you expect to owe in taxes—even when extending your time to file.

All the best to your withholding and wealth building success as you deserve nothing less...

For more information on the topics in this chapter visit the Tax Archive page at:

TheWealthIncreaser.com

Chapter 3 Understanding Tax Brackets

Learn how you can achieve more and build wealth more efficiently by gaining a better understanding of tax brackets...

In the United States, many consumers who are required to file a federal (and state) tax return often find understanding of the system to be difficult, confusing and hard to understand.

However, the system is not as complicated as many think for most taxpayers, and if you file taxes in the U. S., you want to put yourself in a more favorable position so that you can achieve at a higher level of excellence throughout your lifetime!

In this chapter, "the focus on taxes" and how you can gain a better understanding of "tax brackets" so that you can achieve more throughout your lifetime and better prepare for the filing of your taxes in future years so that you can be more successful will be presented in great detail.

You must desire to put forth real effort so that you will sincerely build wealth more effectively, and gaining a real understanding of tax brackets is an important step in helping you improve upon your money management habits.

For you to better follow this chapter, a few terms will be defined below:

Effective tax rate—your effective tax rate would be the rate that you are taxed at from an overall perspective. If you are in the 10, 12 and 22% tax bracket your effective rate would be averaged based on your taxable income and the various tax brackets.

Marginal tax rate—your marginal tax rates are based on your income according to IRS guidelines and they range from 0, 10, 12, 22, 24, 32, 35, and 37%.

Alternative Minimum Tax—if you had very high income and would be able to avoid taxation altogether or at a very low level under the

current tax code, the AMT would come in to ensure that you paid taxes at a minimal level.

Net Investment Income Tax—if you have high income, generally $200,000 and up, you will pay an additional tax of 3.8% on your capital gains after the sale of your assets on your tax return.

Ordinary income—your income, taxed as ordinary income rates based on your marginal tax rates mentioned above.

Capital gain—sale of an asset at a gain, usually taxed at the more favorable rate of 0, 15, or 20% which is normally lower than the ordinary income tax rate of many who sell assets.

Dividend—a payment made by corporations to shareholders of record, not all companies pay dividends.

Qualified dividend—a dividend that is taxed at the capital gains rates of 0, 15, or 20%, and is generally more favorable to taxpayers.

Qualified Business Income—taxation on a portion of your pass-through income can possibly be avoided if you qualify for the Qualified Business Income (pun intended) deduction.

Modified Adjusted Gross Income—income on your tax return after certain adjustments are made, those adjustments will generally lower your taxable income and could put you in a more favorable position for credits, deductions and a lower amount of taxation.

Taxable income—is income that is subject to taxation after all your adjustments, deductions and credits have been entered generally.

Mileage rate—a rate that is paid for business, medical, charitable travel etcetera that is adjusted annually. The rates differ with the highest going to business mileage.

Standard deduction—the deduction outlined by the IRS that is of a set amount, and is usually adjusted upward annually due to inflation. If the amount is higher than if you were to itemize, you will generally choose the standard deduction, however there are exceptions when itemized may be a better option even when the itemized amount is lower than the standard deduction, so be sure you have a highly competent tax professional to guide you along.

Itemized deduction—deductions that you can take on your tax return have the potential to increase your tax refund or reduce the amount that you owe if the amount is higher than the standard deduction mentioned above. The deductions available among others include—medical, taxes, mortgage interest, and charitable contributions.

Exemption—personal exemptions are no longer allowed on tax returns as a result of the TCJA of 2017.

Form W-4—you can complete a W-4 form and claim dependents, credits and additional amounts that you want to withhold so that you can avoid underpayment of taxes or get a larger refund.

The tax system in the United States is pay as you go, and if you fail to do so, you will be penalized—and that will force you to be in the know.

Estimated taxes—are taxes paid over the course of the tax season, usually on, April 15, June 15, September 15, and January 15 of the new year. By paying the right amount or at least being in the ballpark area, you can avoid the penalty for failure to pay your taxes and stay in good standing with the IRS.

Credits—an advantage to you when you qualify that has the effect of reducing your taxes dollar for dollar, thereby providing a bigger refund or the paying of less in taxes. Always realize that credits are better than deductions.

Deductions—an advantage for you on your taxes that are not dollar for dollar but based on a percentage of your taxable income. They can also provide a bigger refund or the paying of less in taxes for you at tax time.

Dependent

A dependent is generally a qualifying child or relative who relies on you for financial support. To claim a dependent for tax credits or deductions, the dependent must meet specific

requirements outlined by the IRS. You cannot claim yourself as a dependent.

The above definitions are _the author's take_*, for a more technical definition of the tax terms, you may want to utilize your favorite search engine on the world wide web!*

Most who file income taxes in the United States will pay taxes based on their tax rate that is based on their income. Their "marginal tax rate" would be where their income tops off at and is based on tax rates and schedules that come out annually.

Your "effective tax rate" effectively combines all the rates and averages out the rates to give you an effective tax rate, which is the actual amount of taxes percentage wise, that you would be paying based on your income.

By studying the following bullet points, you will see the tax rates in effect for the 2025 tax year. Keep in mind that the numbers adjust annually due to inflation and market activity.

For the **tax year 2025**, the top marginal tax rates are:

Standard deductions. For **single taxpayers and married individuals filing separately for tax year 2025, the standard deduction rises to $15,000** for 2025, an increase of $400 from 2024. For **married couples filing jointly, the standard deduction rises to $30,000**, an increase of $800 from tax year 2024. For **heads of households, the standard deduction will be $22,500** for tax year 2025, an increase of $600 from the amount for tax year 2024.

Marginal rates. For tax year 2025, the top tax rate remains **37% for individual single taxpayers with incomes greater than $626,350 ($751,600 for married couples filing jointly).**

The other rates are:

- **35%** for incomes over $250,525 ($501,050 for married couples filing jointly).

- **32%** for incomes over $197,300 ($394,600 for married couples filing jointly).

- **24%** for incomes over $103,350 ($206,700 for married couples filing jointly).

- **22%** for incomes over $48,475 ($96,950 for married couples filing jointly).

- **12%** for incomes over $11,925 ($23,850 for married couples filing jointly).

- **10%** for incomes $11,925 or less ($23,850 or less for married couples filing jointly.

Note: Income for taxation at the above rates are based on taxable income for the year, not your gross income for the year!

Alternative **M**inimum **T**ax **Exemption Amounts**

For tax year 2025, the exemption amount for unmarried individuals increases to $88,100 ($68,650 for married individuals filing separately) and begins to phase out at $626,350. For married couples filing jointly, the exemption amount increases to $137,000 and begins to phase out at $1,252,700.

Earned **I**ncome **C**redits

For qualifying taxpayers who have three or more qualifying children, **the tax year 2025 maximum Earned Income Tax Credit** amount is $8,046, an increase from $7,830 for tax year 2024. The revenue procedure contains a table providing maximum EITC amount for other categories, income thresholds and phase-outs.

Qualified transportation fringe benefit

For tax year 2025, the monthly limitation for the qualified transportation fringe benefit and the monthly limitation for qualified parking rises to $325, increasing from $315 in tax year 2024.

ABLE Accounts

The **A**chieving a **B**etter **L**ife **E**xperience (ABLE) **Act of 2014** allows states to create tax-advantaged savings programs for eligible people with disabilities (designated beneficiaries). Funds from these **529A ABLE**

accounts can help designated beneficiaries pay for qualified disability expenses. Distributions are tax-free if used for qualified disability expenses.

Health flexible spending cafeteria plans

For the taxable years beginning in 2025, the dollar limitation for employee salary reductions for contributions to health **f**lexible **s**pending **a**rrangements rises to $3,300, increasing from $3,200 in tax year 2024.

For cafeteria plans that permit the carryover of unused amounts, the maximum carryover amount rises to $660, increasing from $640 in tax year 2024.

Health **S**avings **A**ccounts or **HSA**

For tax year 2025, participants who have self-only coverage the plan **must have an annual deductible that is not less than $2,850** (a $50 increase from the previous tax year), **but not**

more than $4,300 (an increase of $150 from the previous tax year).

The maximum out-of-pocket expense amount rises to $5,700, increasing from $5,550 in tax year 2024.

For **family coverage** in tax year 2025, the annual deductible is **not less than $5,700**, increasing from $5,550 in tax year 2024; however, **the deductible cannot be more than $8,550**, an increase of $200 versus the limit for tax year 2024.

For family coverage, the out-of-pocket expense limit is $10,500 for tax year 2025, rising from $10,200 in tax year 2024.

Foreign earned income exclusion

For tax year 2025, the foreign earned income exclusion increases to $130,000, from $126,500 in tax year 2024.

Estate tax credits

Estates of decedents who die during 2025 have a basic exclusion amount of $13,990,000, increased from $13,610,000 for estates of decedents who died in 2024.

Gift Tax Exclusion

Annual exclusion for gifts **increases to $19,000 for calendar year 2025**, rising from $18,000 for calendar year 2024.

Adoption credits

For tax year 2025, the maximum credit allowed for the adoption of a child with special needs is the amount of qualified adoption expenses up to $17,280, increased from $16,810 for tax year 2024.

Unchanged for tax year 2025 by statute, certain items that were indexed for inflation in the past are currently not adjusted.

- **Personal exemptions** for tax year 2025 remain at 0, as in tax year 2024. The elimination of personal exemptions was a provision in the **T**ax **C**uts and **J**obs **A**ct of 2017.

- **Itemized deductions**. There is no limitation on itemized deductions for tax year 2025, as in tax year 2024 and preceding, to tax year 2018. The limitation on itemized deductions was eliminated by the **T**ax **C**uts and **J**obs **A**ct of 2017.

- **Lifetime learning credits.** The modified adjusted gross income amount used by taxpayers to determine the reduction in the **L**ifetime **L**earning **C**redit provided in Sec. 25A(d)(1) of the Internal Revenue Code is not adjusted for inflation for taxable years beginning after Dec. 31, 2020. The Lifetime Learning Credit is phased out for taxpayers with modified adjusted gross income more than $80,000 ($160,000 for joint returns).

Conclusion or Key Points

Always remember that tax brackets adjust annually, and you want to have an idea of how your income is taxed and at what **marginal** and **effective** tax rate, so that you can compare from year to year and use analysis to not only plan better, but also implement those plans more effectively and efficiently to help you achieve the goals that you desire in a more time certain manner.

Your tax professional should be able to provide you with **comparison data** (and explain the data) from year to year on your "marginal" and "effective" tax rates that you pay so that you can use the data to your advantage in future years.

If your marginal tax rate is 22% and your effective tax rate is 13.4%, you want to know that—as by knowing you can gauge what you are paying tax wise as compared to others in your society and use the numbers to plan for your tax payment and earnings in future years based on realistic data! If you pay state taxes, you also want to know the marginal and effective tax rates from year-to-year as well.

Effective tax management <u>**plays an important role**</u> in your overall wealth building success, and it is important that you at a minimum <u>learn the basics about tax brackets</u>, as taxation in various forms are here to stay.

Always remember, if you don't <u>contribute to the solution</u> by <u>managing your taxes and finances more effectively</u>, your lack of engagement is normally the main problem that is preventing you from <u>achieving more</u> during your lifetime.

Your ability to comprehend and understand **tax brackets** can <u>put you in position for a lifetime of success</u> for those who live in the U.S., and for those who are willing to give it their absolute best.

By understanding and applying at a minimum what you have learned from <u>tax basics</u>, <u>**tax brackets**</u>, <u>tax withholdings</u> and what you will soon learn about in the next chapter on **filing status**, you will put yourself well ahead of the average taxpayer, however you want to be more than just ahead—

your goal is to give it your absolute best so that you will achieve ultimate success as you put procrastination to rest.

All the best as you reach higher to achieve the goals that you truly desire, and at the same time put yourself in position to avoid a financial and tax quagmire.

Chapter 4 Filing Status & Exactly Who is a Dependent

Learn about the various tax filing options so that you can build wealth more efficiently…

Over the years, many have posed questions and concerns about their filing status and who qualifies as a dependent. In this chapter you will have the opportunity to clear up some of the misunderstandings that you and others may have as it relates to "filing status and claiming" of dependents.

Even though filing and dependent statuses can get highly technical for some, it is fairly straight-forward for most!

As a taxpayer, you need to know that your filing status in future years will be based on your circumstances.

According to the IRS, there are ***five filing statuses*** *that include:*

Single

Head Of Household

Married Filing Jointly

Married Filing Separately

Qualifying Widow(er)

Single

If you are single and have no dependents you would file as single. It is generally one of the simplest returns to file as you are only including your income, adjustments, deductions and credits that apply to you only, however there are exceptions as you might expect as all tax filing situations are unique.

If you are single and have a child that you provide majority support for, you can generally claim the child (assuming the other parent isn't qualified to do so) and that could put you in position to file as **HOH** and that could lead to you claiming a higher standard deduction, qualify you for tax credits such as the child tax credit, earned income credit, and possibly other credits.

2024 Single filing thresholds:

Under 65
$14,600

65 or older **$16,550**

If you are also a homeowner, you may qualify for additional tax savings as you may be able to avoid utilizing the standard deduction and claim itemized deductions instead!

Head Of Household

Head of household is generally a more advantageous filing status for those who qualify, compared to other filing statuses except for **MFJ**, and possibly **QW**.

If you have qualifying dependents, you are eligible to file as HOH, generally.

If your income thresholds are less than the numbers below, you may not have to file, however if you want a refund of tax withholding and the benefits of credits and deductions that may allow you to get a refund—you want to take advantage of that opportunity.

2024 HOH filing thresholds:

under 65 $21,900

65 or older $23,850

If you are also a homeowner, you may qualify for additional tax savings as you may be able to avoid utilizing the standard deduction and claim itemized deductions instead!

Married Filing Jointly

Married couples often find it more advantageous to file jointly, and filing is required if the following income thresholds are met:

2024 MFJ filing thresholds:

under 65 (both spouses)	**$29,200**
65 or older (one spouse)	**$30,750**
65 or older (both spouses)	**$32,300**

If you are married and also a homeowner, you may qualify for additional tax savings!

Married Filing Separately

Married Filing Separately is often used by those who are separated in marriage. In other cases happily married couples seeking relief from taxes due to innocent spouse or injured spouse claims of one taxpayer can often file MFS and that can often be a wise move, as it can lead to less taxes being paid by one spouse, and in many cases lowers the overall taxes that they would pay if they were to file as MFJ.

The IRS considers a couple married for tax filing purposes until they get a final decree of divorce, or a separate maintenance agreement is in effect.

The filing threshold is as follows for **2024 MFS** filers:

any age $5—yes $5!

Qualifying Widow(er)

2024 QW filing thresholds:

under 65 $29,200

65 or older $30,750

The term qualified widow or widower refers to a tax filing status that allows a surviving spouse to use the married filing jointly tax rates on an individual return.

The provision is good for up to two years following the death of one spouse. The taxpayer must remain unmarried for at least two years following the death of their spouse to qualify for this status.

2025 Tax Filing Threshholds:

Single	under 65	$15,000
Single	65 or older	$17,000
Head of Household	under 65	$22,500
Head of Household	65 or older	$24,500

Married Filing Jointly	under 65 (both spouses)	$30,000
Married Filing Jointly	65 or older (one spouse)	$31,600
Married Filing Jointly	65 or older (both spouses)	$33,200
Married Filing Separately	any age	$5
Qualifying Surviving Spouse	under 65	$30,000
Qualifying Surviving Spouse	65 or older	$31,600

Visit Internal Revenue Service "Filing Status" at IRS.gov to learn more.

You must file an income tax return for a decedent (a person who died) if both of the following are true.

1. Your spouse died, or you are the executor, administrator, or legal representative.

2. The decedent met the filing requirements based on the amounts listed above at the time of the decedent's death—or if after 2024 tax year the amount that is in effect during the tax year of decedents death.

For more information, see *Final Income Tax Return for Decedent—Form 1040 or 1040-SR* in Pub. 559.

Form 1310 may also need to be filed so that you can stay in good standing with the IRS!

MFJ vs MFS

Many married tax filers want to know whether it is more advantageous to file separately. You can determine which way **is** more advantageous by running the numbers (or have your tax professional do so).

That's because there are more tax deductions and credits married couples filing jointly are eligible for. For example, the **E**arned **I**ncome **T**ax **C**redit is generally only available to married couples who file jointly. The **EITC** enables low-income households to recoup as much as $7,430 (2024 tax year) and up to $8,046 (2025 tax year) off their taxes if they have three or more children (it is a refundable credit based on earned income).

Similarly, the Adoption Credit and Child and Dependent Care Tax Credit are only available for married couples filing jointly. These and other credits that you may be eligible for can directly lower your tax bill and result in bigger refunds.

Also, if you don't owe any money to the IRS but your spouse does, by filing together your tax refund could be applied toward the tab that your spouse racked up with the IRS.

The 7.5% medical deduction that you can claim on schedule A may be available to one income, but with two incomes you wouldn't qualify based on the 7.5% income threshold.

It is Important that you realize that filing jointly means you and your spouse are on the hook for the money you and your spouse owe to the IRS prior to your marriage.

As far as tax return retention, you want to keep your tax return for a minimum of 3 years, and if you are a homeowner you want to keep all your tax returns permanently!

1098-E student loan interest deduction for those who have student loans are deductible whether you itemize or claim the standard deduction.

Dependents

Many want to know who qualifies as a dependent and who they can legally claim on their current year tax return. It is a common question that unsurprisingly deserves a common answer.

Who qualifies as a dependent, depends (no pun intended)?

Generally, if your income is $5,050 or less you may be able to be claimed by another as a dependent on their return.

However, there are other situations when filing is required that can get quite technical. Additionally in some cases if you are claimed as a dependent by another, you can still file your own tax return utilizing the standard deduction only, as your dependency ~~exemption~~ (credit) has already been used up.

General rules for dependents

These rules generally apply to all dependents:

- A dependent must be a U.S. citizen, resident alien or national or a resident of Canada or Mexico

- A person can't be claimed as a dependent on more than one tax return, with rare exceptions

- A dependent can't claim a dependent on their own tax return

- You can't claim your spouse as a dependent if you file jointly

- You can't claim yourself as a dependent

- A dependent must be a qualifying child or qualifying relative

Qualifying child

To qualify as a dependent, a child must also pass these tests:

- Relationship: Be your son, daughter, stepchild, eligible foster child, brother, sister, half-sister or -brother, stepbrother, stepsister, adopted child or the child of one of these
- Age: Be under age 19 **or** under 24 if a full-time student, **or** any age if permanently and totally disabled
- Residency: Live with you for more than half the year, with some exceptions
- Support: Get more than half their financial support from you
- Joint return: Not file as married filing jointly unless only to claim a refund of taxes paid or withheld

See the full rules for a qualifying child at IRS.gov

Qualifying relative

A qualifying relative must meet general rules for dependents and pass these tests:

- Not a qualifying child: Isn't your qualifying child or the qualifying child of any other taxpayer
- Member of household or relationship: Lives with you all year as a member of your household or is a specific type of relative
- Gross income: Has gross income under $5,050
- Support: Gets more than half their financial support from you

See the full rules for a qualifying relative at IRS.gov

When can I claim a dependent?

You can currently claim dependents only for certain tax credits and deductions.

Each credit or deduction has its own requirements!

- **Child Tax Credit**
- **Adoption expenses**
- **Additional Child Tax Credit**
- **Credit for Other Dependents**
- **Earned Income Tax Credit (EITC)**
- **Child and Dependent Care Credit**
- **Education credits**
- **Medical expense deductions**
- **Other itemized deductions**

What if I am a "dependent" on someone else's return?

You can be claimed as a dependent and still need to file your own tax return. Your filing requirement depends on your income, marital status and other criteria.

Learn more by visiting more details on filing requirements for dependents at IRS.gov.

<u>To see if you need to file a federal tax return: answer questions to find out at irs.gov website.</u>

Always remember that even though you may not be required to file, you may want to file (federal and state returns) anyway so you can get any federal and state income tax your employer withheld back as a refund or claim certain <u>refundable or non-refundable tax credits that you qualify for.</u>

You also want to be aware of the more stringent “due diligence guidelines” that tax professionals must follow as they are required to document information that you provide in order to verify your eligibility for certain adjustments, credits, and deductions.

Dependents, Standard Deduction, and Filing Information, Publication 501 that can be found at IRS.gov provides more information.

Your Federal Income Tax, Publication 17, a "must read" for those who sincerely desire to succeed could also be helpful.

What Triggers an Audit?

To conclude this chapter on filing status, audit triggers will be presented to help you gain a better understanding of filing requirements and how to avoid unnecessary IRS scrutiny so that you can achieve more in the coming tax seasons.

Among other tax concerns, you want to be particularly aware of common audit triggers.

Common Audit Triggers include the following:

- **Under-reporting taxable income**—retirement, side jobs, 401k loan non-repayment, 1099 or other income not being reported can all lead to under-reporting of income, which the IRS frowns upon

- **Claiming large or unusual deductions**—business expenses, charitable contributions and the like

- **Significant changes from year to year**—if you have major changes from your previous tax return, that may cause alarm at the IRS

- **Independent contractor or self-employment income not reported**—Venmo, air b-n-b, VRBO, lyft, UBER, Turo, Grubhub, Doordash, Roadie and other new economy ways of making income are normally taxable, and the IRS normally receives 1099-k or other 1099s from the platforms or app providers

- **Claiming credits that they don't qualify for**—i.e. the EIC, Dependent Credit, CTC etcetera

Keep in mind the IRS has matching computer system technology that allows them to cross-reference and easily detect many discrepancies in tax reporting.

Therefore, you want to keep good records and stay abreast of reporting requirements!

Additionally, you want to file your tax return annually, and if you need additional time you want to file form 4868, as that will give you an additional six months to get your finances and payment options in place.

Likewise, you want to timely file your tax return if you are due a refund as there are limitations in place that would disallow your refund if not done within a 3-year period from the filing deadline—including extensions.

If you have "security concerns" about your taxes, you want to give an **IP PIN** real consideration as an Individual Protection Personal Identification Number can provide added security by providing you a **PIN (P**ersonal **I**dentification **N**umber**)** on an annual basis that requires two-factor verification—thus decreasing the likelihood of fraud occurring against you and your family.

Always be aware of phishing and spoofing and the use of Artificial Intelligence as there is a substantial increase in the use of these techniques that are designed to get your tax and financial data and assets, therefore use extreme caution as the IRS and other creditors have no need to ask you about data that they should already have on file. Never give out personally identifiable information or financial data online or over the phone unless you are absolutely certain—and even then, it may not be wise to do so.

Conclusion or Key Points

Your filing status and determining who is a "dependent" is generally easy to determine, however on occasion, determining the best filing status or who qualifies as a dependent can be difficult and may require analysis, including doing pro-forma projections using varying filing statuses that you may qualify for.

Even on occasions when you are not required to file, you may want to do so if you had taxes withheld as you may be able to get some or all the withholding back along with additional amounts—depending on your circumstances.

Additionally, you may qualify for deductions and refundable credits, therefore by not filing you could be leaving money on the table. You also want to take your state and local taxes into consideration when deciding your filing status, as even if you qualify at the federal level and do not have to file, you may be required to do so at the state or local level.

In general, your filing status should be easy to decipher, however those who qualify as a dependent may need to be given deeper analysis in some situations!

And with filing status and dependents, and many other areas of taxation, you want to be aware of the ever-changing nature of taxation along with the increased use of AI (**A**rtificial **I**ntelligence) and other techniques around tax fraud.

You want to know proactively that credits, deductions, mileage rates and adjustment ceilings or deductible contribution limits such as on IRAs—change from year to year (usually of an upward nature), therefore you want to be highly conscious and aware of this important fact—as you want to see what numbers are in effect for the current tax year or the year in question (the tax year that you are filing) so that you can improve your analysis and decision making and build wealth more efficiently.

If you have major concerns, you want to do additional research and/or contact a highly competent tax professional to assist you in the process. Always remember that a marriage, birth, death, divorce, adoption or the claiming of a parent or other qualifying dependent(s) that occurs by December 31st of the tax year in question has the potential to change your filing status for the current tax year or future tax year(s).

In the case of death during the tax year by the primary taxpayer, an executor or personal representative may have to file final return of a decedent, as tax obligations are "not" relieved—even in death. If not done appropriately you, as the executor or personal representative, can be held personally liable.

After the transition of the primary taxpayer (or spouse), **MFJ** tax rates are still an option when filing, and **QW** can be done in future years (for a two-year period after transition). Therefore, it is important that you look at your circumstances in a wholesome way and determine the best way to file.

As the primary taxpayer (or spouse of primary taxpayer), you don't want to pass on to your surviving spouse debt that you incurred while you were alive if you can avoid it. With married couples, both parties are singularly or jointly obligated.

Tax obligations of your spouse can be paid through the estate or through you, therefore your filing status election and estate planning could be key to you saving money and building wealth more efficiently.

Always realize that once your estate is opened after your transition, the IRS generally gets paid first!

Isn't it time you get a real GRIP on your taxes and finances so that you can ascend higher and do more of what you sincerely desire.

And with all of the economic disarray—now is the time that you finally put your filing status and other tax concerns at bay so that life can go your way!

Even though the current economy is in upheaval, you don't have to pursue your goals in error because of the actions of others who are evil.

All the best to your filing status success as you work diligently during these tumultuous times to give it your absolute best...

To learn more about filing status and dependents visit: Tax Archive—TheWealthIncreaser.com

Chapter 5 Hot Tax Topics

Learn about some of the latest tax news so that you can avoid the tax blues...

In this chapter you will learn a "number of critical areas of tax understanding" that could help you maximize your tax position from this day forward. Furthermore, you will learn about many common tax concerns that a vast number of "tax filers" have had over the years.

To achieve more and maximize your personal income tax return it is important that you have knowledge of—and a practical understanding of how you can do the following more effectively:

Use the New Tax Rates to Your Advantage

If you are an individual and do not have majority ownership in a C corporation or S Corporation–your maximum tax rate is 37% versus the maximum for a corporation of 21%, due to the job and tax act of 2017.

That means if you have high income that puts you in the upper income tax brackets you could possibly reduce the taxation of your income by establishing a corporation or keeping your income in the corporation as opposed to receiving a salary if you now have a corporation.

There are several ways that you can strategize to lower your taxes by using the new tax rates to your advantage and it is up to you and your professional team to find ways to do just that.

If you are a business owner or desire to be one, you must understand the forms of ownership!

- **Sole Proprietorship**
- **Limited Liability Company (LLC)**
- **Limited Liability Partnership (LLP)**
- **S Corporation**
- **C Corporation**

You must know and understand fully that certain types of ownership allow you to shield your personal assets against the liabilities of your business.

If you are operating as a sole proprietor where you are using your social security number as your Federal ID, you are putting yourself and your family in position to be personally liable for actions that may arise out of liabilities of your business.

Whether a pass through entity or a corporation will be of greatest benefit to you will depend on your unique tax and financial position, the type of business you operate, the state that you are in, your liability (risk) exposure and the path that you desire to take to reach your goals once you lay out all of your intentions, whether you decide yourself—or you decide to use financial professionals.

IRA's

IRA's and other tax favored retirement plans retain those tax advantages despite the **T**ax **C**ut and **J**obs

Act of 2017. That means the "saver's credit" and deductibility for a traditional IRA are still available for those who qualify.

In addition, **ROTH conversions** can be done regardless of your income level and **ROTH IRAs** still enjoy the tax-free benefit upon withdrawal if done so according to IRS guidelines. Contributions remain tax free upon withdrawal.

With both IRA's the first time homebuyer withdrawal provision remains as well as several other "exceptions" that can help you avoid the tax bite if you were to withdraw prematurely.

HSA's

A Health Savings Account may allow you to save more and meet your health care expenses in a tax efficient manner by allowing you to:

1) deduct the amount you contribute
2) allow your contributions to grow tax free, and

3) allow you to withdraw your earnings tax free when used for medical related expenses

Be sure to give the "triple tax benefit" of HSA's real consideration. In addition, be aware of the expenses that you will pay to the provider of the HSA account, as expenses can eat away at your earnings. Be sure to shop for the best plan available based on your financial position and health saving goals.

You also want to know at the earliest time possible if you are going to utilize the standard deduction or itemize your deductions when possible.

Standard Deduction

The **standard deduction** has been increased for the 2018 tax year onward, and many of those who once itemized will find that it is no longer to their advantage to do so.

For single taxpayers and married individuals filing separately **for tax year 2025**, the standard deduction rises to $15,000 for 2025, an increase of $400 from 2024.

For married couples filing jointly, **the 2025** standard deduction rises to $30,000, an increase of $800 from tax year 2024.

For heads of households, the standard deduction will be $22,500 **for tax year 2025**, an increase of $600 from the amount for tax year 2024.

Singles are now at $15,000

Head of Household is now at $22,500

Married Filing Jointly is now at $30,000

Personal exemption eliminated for most—some dependents on your tax return may allow you to claim a $500 dependent credit.

Be sure to consider the effect on your state tax refund or payment in determining whether to itemize or claim the standard deduction—as you may be surprised to find that a reduced itemized deduction at the federal level could still be to your benefit if you would get a higher overall refund or pay less in taxes when the federal and state amounts have been combined!

Itemized Deductions:

Medical

Long-Term Care (LTC) insurance that you pay, Medical Insurance that you pay, Health Care Insurance Premiums that you pay, Eye Care that you received during the year, Out of Pocket medical expenses that you pay for the year, Dental Expenses that you pay for the year, Prescription drugs that you purchase for the year, Mileage to and from your medical care destination and many other medical related expenses may all be deductible in 2025 if they exceed 7.5% of your AGI (Adjusted Gross Income–line 11 on page 1 of form 1040) and you itemize your deductions.

The AGI limit increased to 10% in 2019, however as of 2025 tax year it is at 7.5%.

Taxes

State income taxes and sales taxes, ad valorem taxes, property taxes and possibly other taxes may be deductible by you if you itemize and otherwise qualify.

Keep in mind that there are limitations on taxes in some instances—so keep that in mind—particularly if you are in a high tax state such as California, New York, New Jersey, Connecticut and several others.

Mortgage Interest

Mortgage interest deduction is now limited to $750,000 down from 1 million.

Mortgage Insurance Premiums **(MIP)** and Private Mortgage Insurance **(PMI)** are not deductible for the 2025 tax year and beyond unless Congress acts.

Charitable Contributions

New rules apply to deducting charitable contributions that are non-cash as you must provide additional documentation for donations valued over $250.

As for church donations and others that are in the form of cash, the maximum percentage that you can deduct has changed, however the required documentation is basically the same.

2% AGI Deductions Eliminated

Tax related fees, investment fees, **unreimbursed employee expenses** (including automobile expenses) and other 2% of AGI deductions, have been eliminated for 2018 through 2025 tax years.

Social Security Income Threshold Increases

In tax year 2018 the maximum social security wage base was $128,500—however for the 2025 tax year, that wage base will increase to $176,100 which means if you earned over $176,100 in 2025 you won't pay a tax on the income over that amount (6.2% of the amount up to $176,100 will be taxed) when you file your 2025 taxes, the Medicare payment portion of 2.90% is still applicable however.

The Medicare portion limit did not change because of the tax cut and jobs act of 2017 as there is no limit.

Although planning proactively and keeping your tax filing current is usually the best approach to staying in good standing with the IRS, many may currently owe the IRS, and if that is you—you have options.

If you find yourself in the unfortunate position of **owing the IRS**, particularly if it is $10,000 or more, you have options that include the following among others:

Offer-in-Compromise—An offer in compromise **(form 656 along with form 433A and/or 433B)** may allow you to settle your tax debt for less than the full amount you owe. Your financial information and tax filing status can be used to see if you qualify for an **OIC**, and if you qualify you could see a reduction in the amount that you owe the IRS.

You would include your **current filing information, assets, income, expenses and a proposed settlement amount** to the IRS and if they accepted you would have a time frame to come up with the settlement amount. An application fee and initial payment are also normally required. You would normally have 2 payment options:

Lump Sum: This option requires 20% of the total offer amount to be paid with the offer and the remaining balance paid in 5 or fewer payments within 5 months of the date your offer is accepted.

Periodic Payment: This option requires you to make the first payment with the offer and the remaining balance paid in monthly payments within 6 to 24 months, in accordance with your proposed offer terms.

Installment Agreement—If you owe $50,000 or less, you may be able to use the **form 9465** to request a monthly installment plan if you cannot pay the full amount of tax that you owe. You must be current on all your tax filings to make this a successful request.

Temporary Delay in Collection—A job loss or reduction in income, a federal disaster declaration in your area and other hardships could allow you to file **form 433** to buy you time, as it would allow the IRS to designate what you owe as currently not collectible. Keep in mind penalties and interest may accrue, and the IRS may file a "federal tax lien" against your property to protect their interests.

If any of the above strategies are used, you may be able to stay in good standing with the IRS or "buy time" so that you can make arrangements to stay current or pay off your income tax tabulation. With all the options listed above technicalities apply, and you will have to meet those technicalities to qualify for the payoff plan.

Always Realize the IRS has the Power to Place a Lien or Levy on Property You Own!

It is important that you distinguish a tax lien from a tax levy, as a lien **is not** a levy.

A lien **secures the IRS's interest in your property** when you don't pay your tax debt.

A levy **actually takes the property to pay the tax debt,** and if you don't pay or make arrangements to settle your tax debt, the IRS can levy, seize and sell any type of real or personal property that you own or have an interest in.

Current Trends

It is important that you realize that we are not in normal times as trade wars, tariffs, inflation and unusual market activity are causing concern for many.

Uncertainty in the markets in the **spring of 2025** even caused bond prices to go down! Stagflation is now a real concern as the potential for a combination of high inflation, stagnant economic growth, and elevated unemployment appears to be a real possibility.

If you are considering the purchase of a new or move-up home, be aware in advance of the $750,000 "mortgage interest limitation" or you will have to pro-rate interest **(form 14900)** if your mortgage loan exceeds that amount.

You want to know from this day forward that documentation and substantiation of tax matters are critical for you if you want to increase your tax savings and stay in good standing with the IRS.

It is imperative that you have a good organization system in place, and you properly track business expenses, assets, charitable contributions, mileage in all forms, and other tax, financial or business-related activities that have the potential to come under scrutiny by the IRS.

Conclusion or Key Points

It is important that you realize that many changes have occurred over the past few years as they relate to your taxes and the filing of your tax return and the potential for major changes in the future are always a possibility.

The **form 1040** has a new look and now includes **"Schedules"** that allow you to include in income or deduct many of the items that were on **page 1 of the 1040.**

1040EZ and 1040A no longer exist and you must use form 1040 to file your 2018 through 2025 tax returns.

In most instances you won't claim exemptions, however the child tax credit has gone up to $2,000 per child with up to $1,700 of the credit refundable. A Dependent credit of $500 is now available for tax filers who qualify.

Student loan interest deduction and other educational credits remain.

Whether it is the "Affordable Health Care Act" (penalty was eliminated after the 2018 tax filing year) the "Tax Cut and Jobs Act of 2017" , the "Inflation Reduction Act" of 2022, or any other incidental changes in the tax code that will occur in future years, it is important that you put yourself and your family in position to take advantage of the changes and not let the changes take advantage of you.

Be sure to choose highly competent professionals and be sure to gain the knowledge that you need so that you can succeed.

Be sure to engage with professionals who have a track record of success, someone who encourages you to ask questions and are willing to spend the time that is necessary so that you can fully understand the answers to the questions that you ask–and someone who adds value to your financial and overall life from this day forward!

You want to put yourself in an informed position where you know what is going on "tax wise" so that you can position yourself in a way where you can't easily be taken advantage of.

By purchasing this book alone—you are showing a real commitment toward success in your future and you are on a path to maximizing your tax knowledge in a way that will put you and your family in position to achieve more throughout your lifetime.

By purchasing this book, you have put yourself in position to not be easily taken advantage of like many were during the financial crisis that occurred in 2008!

You will put yourself in position to know how the recent tax changes over the past few years or future tax changes will affect you and your family—thus giving you the opportunity to plan proactively and improve the likelihood that you will achieve your goals.

You will know how to respond to tariffs and other market activity from a better vantage point.

You no longer must let your **i**gnorance of the tax laws, **i**mmaturity in approaching your finances, **i**nsecurity in approaching your finances or the **i**nability to approach your finances due to fear–lead to **i**dleness and not moving forward in the financial realm of your life!

Today is the day that the Five "I's" die—and you more than just try!

Today is the day that you pursue a new road to success that has fewer turns, and less stress and moves your forward in a way that allows you to give it your very best!

Today is the day that you become aware, mature, believe in yourself, operate daily with character and move to action in a manner where the success that you see has already been achieved.

All the best to your new tax knowledge and new journey toward success…

Chapter 6 Understanding Capital Gains

Learn more about capital gains and how they are taxed so that you can efficiently build wealth...

Even with all that is happening with tariffs and uncertainty on the world stage, there are some bright spots when it comes to paying taxes in the United States.

Although there is much that is simple and uneventful in the tax code, there also are more complex topics that could be more challenging for you when it comes to using the tax code to your benefit and you want to be aware of them proactively as opposed to re-actively.

Whether it is the sale of your home and the exclusion of gain, ($500,000 married and $250,000 single if you qualify), using Depreciation/Mileage, using Retirement Deductions/Savers Credit, Schedule A Deductions along with numerous other deductions that may appear complex but could be of real benefit to you at this time or at a time in your future, if you qualify or potentially qualify—you want to know about them.

Therefore, you want to be aware of them "prior to" filing your tax return—<u>not after</u> so that you can reach your <u>immediate, short-term, intermediate and long-term goals</u> in a more satisfying manner!

Just so we are all on the same page, a few terms will be defined so that you can comprehend this chapter with more clarity:

<u>Interest</u>—a charge for borrowed money generally a percentage of the amount borrowed.

<u>Deferral of gain</u>—in a tax-deferred exchange, the deferred gain is the amount of gain that escapes current taxation and is deferred until a later date. Deferral of gain is a strategy that is often used in 1031 exchanges involving like-kind property by savvy investors who desire not to pay taxes at the time, and/or desire to prolong the payment of capital gain taxes to a date in the future and in some cases after they transition.

Depreciation Recapture—when you sell a rental property for more than its original purchase price, the sale price gets split into two parts. FIRST, any profit up to the amount of depreciation you've

claimed in previous years gets the maximum 25% recapture rate. The remainder is taxed at your capital gains rate of 0, 15 or 20% depending on your taxable income. There is also a possibility that NIIT could come into play, depending on your income.

Dividends—a dividend is a distribution of a company's earnings to eligible shareholders (not all companies pay dividends).

ESOP—stock options offered to employees at some companies.

Ordinary dividend—ordinary income is income earned by an entity or an individual that is taxable at marginal tax rates, therefore an ordinary dividend that you received would be taxed at your marginal tax rate.

Qualified dividend—a qualified dividend is an ordinary dividend reported to the Internal Revenue Service (IRS), which taxes it at capital gains tax rates which are generally more favorable to most taxpayers.

Realized gain—a real profit that shows up not only on paper, but also in your bank or investment account. A "realized gain" is an increase in the value of an asset or investment you own and have sold or cashed in on.

A tax occurs on a realized gain only when sold and if held for over a year the gain would be taxed at the capital gains rate based on your income. Exceptions may apply in certain situations based on the asset classification, timing of the gain, depreciation, and your income level as the AMT or NIIT could apply, thus increasing the taxation on the gain.

Unrealized gain—a potential profit that shows up on paper or an increase in value of an asset or investment you may own but have not sold or cashed in on. A tax occurs only when sold.

Realized and unrealized losses also follow the same logic, as there is either a paper loss or an actual loss, depending on the actions you take or fail to take and at what time you take those actions (short versus long-term).

Capital asset—capital assets among others include stocks, bonds, mutual funds, 529 plans, real estate, sale of business, crypto, timber sales from your land, collectibles, etcetera. Capital assets are significant pieces of property such as homes, cars, investment properties, stocks, bonds, mutual funds, ETFs and even collectibles or art.

Although there are exceptions, capital gains can be short (taxed as ordinary income) or long term (taxed at the generally more favorable capital gains rate of 0, 15, or 20%) and deferred as in the case of a "successful" 1031 exchange or installment sale!

In many instances you will have to pay capital gains taxes if you sell a capital asset for a gain and in some cases a capital loss can be used to offset capital gains to a limit. In this chapter the topic of capital gains that you can use to achieve more during your lifetime will be covered in detail.

Common "exceptions" to standard capital gain rates:

***Collectibles* (taxed at the higher 28% rate)**

***Owner Occupied Real Estate* (all or a portion may be excluded from taxation depending on the amount of gain)**

***Rental Real Estat*e (depreciation add back may increase your capital gains tax)**

***1031 exchange* (a successful exchange can defer your taxes to a later date once property is sold)**

***Installment Sale* (instead of being taxed in one year, your gain would be taxed over several years and that could have the effect of lowering or eliminating your overall capital gains tax)**

Capital Gains

Capital gains are different from interest income paid by bonds or those which you would receive from a CD or savings account at your bank. Regardless of the type of bond, any "debt issue" purchased and sold in the "secondary market" will post a capital gain (or loss).

This includes government and municipal issues, as well as corporate debt. Gains and losses on many **bond transactions** are taxed the same way that other securities, such as stocks or mutual funds, are taxed. That is, at the "appropriate" capital gains tax rate.

Series EE and I bonds are taxed differently and will be discussed later in this chapter.

Internal Revenue Service. "Topic No. 409, Capital Gains and Losses."

How to avoid capital gains tax:

1) Hold assets

2) Use tax-advantaged accounts (HSA/FSA 529s, Other)

3) Installment sale (will help reduce your taxes)

4) Offset gains against losses (use tax loss harvesting)

5) Use home sale exclusion

6) Do a 1031 exchange if you qualify

7) Invest inside your retirement account(s)

8) Invest in a tax-efficient index fund (will reduce capital gains tax because movement of stocks/bonds in fund are minimal)

9) Invest in a qualified opportunity zone fund (QOF)

10) Refinance your home or rental property (considered a loan and no capital gains or any taxation on the proceeds, if used for home improvement, interest repayment may be deductible on your tax return)

11) Inherit assets that will receive the more favorable "stepped-up basis" treatment

12) Hire a professional advisor

Art/Collectables capital gain rate is **28%**

Antique Cars capital gain rate is **28%**

All the following are taxed at the higher capital gain rate of 28%:

- Works of art
- Rugs and Antiques
- Metals and gems (gold, silver, platinum, palladium etcetera)
- Stamps and coins
- Alcoholic beverages (fine wines, rare whiskeys, vintage champagnes, craft beers, limited edition spirits etcetera)

Note: Additionally, the IRS reserves the right to classify any other tangible personal property as a collectible for tax purposes.

And there are some limited exceptions for certain metals, gems, and coins.

Additionally, if you have some of the above assets "inside of a fund" in a non-physical form, you might be able to avoid the higher 28% rate.

Essentially, if you sell your collectible for a profit, you will face capital gains tax. As you would expect, the amount you'll owe depends on how long you've held onto the item (short versus long-term).

For short-term holdings of one year or less, any profit is taxed as ordinary income at your marginal federal tax rate.

Long-term gains, on the other hand, are treated differently:

- If you've held the collectible for over a year, you'll be subject to a maximum tax rate of 28%. This rate is higher than the typical long-term capital gains tax rates of 15% or 20%.

- Why is this rate higher? The federal government basically wants to discourage speculation in potentially volatile markets and encourage investments that contribute more directly to economic growth. Also, while the maximum 28% rate for long-term collectible gains exceeds rates for other assets, it's still lower than short-term rates taxed as ordinary income for those in the higher income tax brackets.

- Determining your tax liability on a collectible sale involves a few steps. First, you need to establish "your basis" in the item.

- For purchased collectibles, like silver bars, for example, your basis is generally the original cost plus any associated fees, such as costs for restoration (for hobbyists), expenses for specialized storage (climate-controlled facilities for art and other collectibles), or fees paid to brokers or dealers to obtain the asset.

- If you inherited the collectible, your basis would be its fair market value "at the time" of inheritance (adjusted basis).

Once you've determined your basis, subtract it from the sales price to find your capital gain. This gain is then subject to the appropriate tax rate based on your holding period and income level.

Bonds—varies as municipal bonds may be tax exempt at the federal and possibly state level.

Cancellation of Debt—could in many cases be taxed at your ordinary income tax rate—you and the IRS would receive a 1099-C from the issuer who canceled your debt.

Collectibles—taxed at 28% rate

To report sales for collectibles, use Form 8949. That information is then entered on Schedule D of Form 1040 to calculate and report your overall gains or losses.

Can the marginal rate on collectibles exceed 28%?

The effective tax rate on collectible gains can sometimes exceed 28% due to the net investment income tax (NIIT) and/or the alternative minimum tax or the more commonly known acronym AMT.

- **Net Investment Income tax (NIIT): Depending on your adjusted gross income, you might face a 3.8% net investment income tax on your gains. NIIT is an additional tax on investment income for those with income exceeding specific thresholds (Modified Adjusted Gross Income of $200,000 for single filers and $250,000 for married couples filing jointly).**

*For more information, see **"What is Net Investment Income Tax"** at IRS.gov?*

- ***Alternative Minimum Tax*** **(AMT): If you are subject to the Alternative Minimum Tax (AMT), your effective tax rate could increase as well. Also realize that your state and local taxes can also contribute to a higher overall tax burden when it comes to gains on collectibles and other capital assets.**

Corporate Bonds

Interest earned from corporate bonds are fully taxable at all levels. Because corporate bonds typically have the "greatest risk" of default, they pay the highest interest rates of any bond. Investors who own 100 corporate bonds at $1,000 par value, with each paying 6% annually, can expect to receive $6,000 of taxable "interest income" each year, unless the account was held inside of a retirement account. If corporate bonds are sold in the open market, there could be capital gain involved.

Corporate earnings—taxed as ordinary income at rate of 21%.

Short-term capital gains arise from the sale of assets held for a year or less and are taxed at the corporation's ordinary income tax rate.

Corporate capital gains

Long-term capital gains result from selling assets held for more than a year and are generally taxed at a lower rate. This tax advantage encourages corporations to adopt strategic asset management practices, often opting to hold assets longer which normally strengthens the economy. The type of assets sold also influence capital gain classification. For example, gains from selling depreciable business property, like machinery, may follow different tax rules than gains from investment securities.

Amortization of Bond Premium

The amortizable bond premium refers to the price paid for a bond above its face value.

The premium paid represents part of the cost basis of the bond, can be tax-deductible, and amortized over the lifespan of the bond.

Amortizing the premium can be advantageous since the tax deduction can offset any interest income the bond generates, thus reducing an investor's taxable income.

Are there Tax-Free Bonds?

While investors will pay federal taxes on the interest income from government bonds, they won't owe state and local taxes. Investors in municipal bonds can avoid taxes altogether if they live in the area where the municipal bond is issued.

Series EE and I bonds can be taxed at time bond is cashed in or annually if elected by the bond holder.

What Is a Corporate Bond?

A corporate bond is a type of debt security issued by a corporation and sold to investors to raise capital. In return for the bond purchase, you would be paid interest at either a fixed or variable interest rate.

Bond Treatment on Tax Returns

Bond income is reported alongside any other interest income earned during the year, which may include interest income from savings accounts, money market accounts, certificates of deposit (CDs), and similar type products.

The tax implications for investors in fixed income can vary, according to the type of security that they purchase. If taxable bond income is a main component of your annual taxes, you can consult a certified public accountant (CPA) or other professionals to assist with tax planning strategies that may reduce or eliminate what you owe.

Before investing in a bond fund or any fund, consider the fund's objectives, risks, charges, and expenses and read the prospectus prior to—not after selecting your fund. Also look at **tax-efficiency** as a bond fund and investments inside of a retirement account allow you to defer (postpone) taxes until you begin withdrawals at a future date (during your retirement years if all goes as planned).

Crypto Currency—considered an asset and capital gains would apply. Cryptocurrency is treated as property for tax purposes in the United States, meaning that any profits from selling or using it are subject to capital gains tax.

You must report any taxable events, such as selling or trading crypto or other digital assets, on your tax return. Additionally, if you own cryptocurrency and digital assets you must disclose if you have movement of those assets, along with disclosing if you have foreign holdings when you file your tax return.

ESOP—stock option offered to employees at some companies that may be taxed at capital gain rates when exercised. If done after retirement and depending on the holding period could be taxed at ordinary income or capital gain rates.

Gaming/Gambling—if you file your taxes using schedule A you can deduct your gambling losses (keep good records) up to the extent of your gains, thus reducing your gain that would be taxed at ordinary income rates up to 37%. In many instances you would receive a form W-2G from the issuer (many winnings over $5,000 will have withholdings up to 24%) and the IRS would also receive a copy.

Gold Bullion/Precious Metals—when it comes to tax purposes, the IRS classifies precious metals held in physical form as collectibles, and thus they may potentially be taxed at the maximum collectable capital gains rate of 28 percent.

Government Bonds

The interest from Treasury bills, notes, and bonds are taxable at the federal level but not at the state and local levels. In addition, some U.S. government agency securities, such as those issued by Fannie Mae, are taxable at the federal level but exempt from state and local taxes.

Municipal Bonds

Municipal bonds are generally tax-free at the federal level and may be tax-free at the local or state level if issued and purchased by you in the area that you reside. Often purchased by high-income investors, municipal bonds can mean tax-free investment income when utilized in a strategic manner.

The interest from these bonds is tax free at the federal, state, and local levels, if investors reside in the same state or municipality as the issuers of the bonds. However, those who buy municipal bonds in the secondary market and later sell them for a capital gain may be taxed at ordinary short-term or long-term capital gains rates.

Mutual Funds/ETFs are taxed at a capital gains rate of 0%, 15% and 20%.

NFT's, Cryptro etcetera: are taxed at a capital gains rate of 0%, 15%, and 20%.

Savings Bonds

Savings bonds are issued by governments to the public and are deemed safe investment vehicles with many benefits. U.S. government Series EE savings bonds are free from state and local tax, and the federal taxes on interest income may be deferred until maturity. The Series I savings bond are also free from state and local tax, and taxation at the federal level can be deferred as well!

Series EE and I Bonds—taxed yearly or when you decide to cash it in, generally federal taxes only apply.

Stocks/Bonds sold in the secondary market are generally taxed at a capital gains rate of 0%, 15% and 20%.

Zero-Coupon Bonds

Although they have no stated coupon rate, zero-coupon bond investors must report a prorated portion of "interest" each year as income.

A zero-coupon bond is an investment in debt that does not pay interest but instead trades at a deep discount.

The profit is realized at its maturity date when the bond is redeemed for its full-face value. Always realize that zero-coupon bonds are issued by governments at discounts, and they mature at par values, where the amount of the spread is divided equally among the number of years to maturity. Consequently, zero-coupon bonds are taxed as interest, just like any other original issue discount bond.

529 Plans have no capital gains or ordinary income taxes assessed on money in a 529 Plan and when the money is withdrawn, if it is used for a qualified purpose, there are no taxes due whatsoever.

Because of 529 tax reforms that went into effect on January 1, 2018, plans now allow up to $10,000 per year per beneficiary to be used towards K-12 private school education.

In addition, the SECURE Act changed the 529 Plans' list of qualified purposes to include certain apprenticeship programs, and to allow up to $10,000 to be used (only once, not annually) to reduce student loan debt for the named beneficiary.

The contribution limits for 529 Plans are the same as the federal annual gift tax exclusion, which is $19,000 per donor, per year, as of 2025.

ROTH IRA—"contribution withdrawals" are normally tax free, however earnings are taxable unless 5-year rule and age 59 1/2 rule is met prior to withdrawal, otherwise taxable with penalty unless an exception applied. Mandatory withdrawals are not required at age 73.

Traditional IRA & Retirement Plans—capital gain taxes are normally deferred, early withdrawals (before age 59 1/2) would be taxed as ordinary income and incur a 10% penalty unless an exception applied. Mandatory withdrawals are normally required at age 73.

Other—my assets don't appear in this chapter!

More research may be necessary by you or your financial professional(s) to determine if you must pay capital gains or any other taxes on the asset in question. Additionally, the IRS reserves the right to classify any other tangible personal property as a collectible for tax purposes.

*Due to the importance of real estate in the building of wealth in many households, the **"capital gains implications"** will be discussed in detail below so that you can build wealth more efficiently.*

Capital Gains & Real Estate

Personal rental real estate "2 of 5 rule" not met, 0%, 15% and 20% capital gains rate apply on rental properties sold (depreciation that you claimed or failed to claim as a deduction over your years as a rental owner will be added back thus increasing your gain).

Personal real estate **2 of 5 rule** met, $250,000 exempt from taxation for single tax filers, and $500,000 if married (technicalities apply) will be exempt if your gains don't exceed these limits and you otherwise qualify.

Rental Real Estate 0%, 15% and 20% on rental properties sold (depreciation recapture of 25% will apply to a **portion of** the sales gain).

Sale of Business form 4797, 0%, 15% 20% or other rate may apply depending on time that business or assets are sold along with the depreciation calculation.

Refinance your home or rental property (considered a loan and no capital gains or any taxation), if proceeds are used for home improvement, interest repayment may be deductible on your tax return.

Many people know the basics of the capital gains tax and are aware that gains on the sale of personal or investment property held for more than one year are taxed at favorable capital gains rates of 0%, 15%, or 20%, plus a 3.8% net investment income tax for people with higher incomes, and a possible 25% tax on depreciation recapture, but many are unaware that:

- **The capital gains rates are based on set income thresholds, which are "adjusted annually" for inflation.**

- **For 2025, the 0% rate applies to individuals with taxable income up to $48,350 for single filers, $64,750 for head-of-household filers, and $96,700 for joint filers.**

- **The 15% rate is for individuals with taxable incomes between the 0% and 20% "break points" of $48,351 to $533,400 for single filers, $64,751 to $566,700 for HOH and $96,701 to $600,050 for joint filers.**

- **The 20% rate starts at $533,401 for single filers, $566,701 for head-of-household filers, and $600,051 for joint filers.**

Residential Real Estate

- Compared to long-term gains, the sale of personal or investment property held for one year or less, which are taxed as ordinary income tax rates up to 37%, the 0, 15%, and 20% rates appear quite appealing. There are also "a lot of exceptions" to these general rules, with some major advantages applying to residential real estate that you must be aware of!

- With many residential home sales, the profit isn't even taxed at all! That's because of the home sale exclusion mentioned earlier that is available if you have owned and **lived in your main home for at least two out of the five years** before the sale date. You could avoid capital gains tax on up to $250,000 ($500,000 for joint filers) of your gain from the sale. Any gain above the $250,000 or $500,000 exclusion amounts is taxed at long-term capital gains rates. If you had a loss from the sale of your primary home, "the loss is not" deductible.

Let's say you're married, bought your home in 2005, have a tax basis of $150,000, and are selling the home for $550,000. The entire $400,000 gain is tax-free to you and your spouse (Call me now and let's party—LOL).

Let's now take the same example, but instead of selling your home for $550,000, you sell it for $900,000. The first $500,000 of the gain is tax-free, and the remaining $250,000 is taxed at long-term capital gains rates. (Call me now and let's "really" party—LOL).

- **To determine your gain or loss from the sale of your primary home, you start with the amount of gross proceeds reported in Box 2 of Form 1099-S and subtract selling expenses such as commissions to arrive at the amount realized.**

- You then reduce that figure by your tax basis in the home to come up with your gain or loss.

- To figure the tax basis in your home, start with the original cost, including the mortgage if you financed the purchase, add certain settlement fees and closing costs, plus the cost of any additions as well as improvements that add to the value of your home, prolong its useful life, or adapt it to better uses.

- IRS Publication 523 has some examples of improvements that increase your tax basis in the home and those that don't. Examples of big-ticket items that are added to your basis include adding a room, installing new air-conditioning, renovating a kitchen, finishing a basement, or putting in new landscaping or a pool. Even small-scale capital improvements can increase the basis. These include new doors and windows, duct and furnace work, built-in appliances and water heaters.

- Repairs, maintenance and improvements that are necessary to keep your residence in good condition but don't add value or prolong its life generally will not increase your basis.

- If you claim a tax credit or otherwise receive a subsidy for putting in <u>energy-savings improvements</u> in your home, you must "first reduce the cost of the system by the tax credit or subsidy that you received" before increasing your home's tax basis.

More on the Home Sale Exclusion can be found at IRS.gov: <u>Capital Gains Tax Home Sale Exclusion, What You Need to Know</u>

If you must sell your home early, you may still be eligible for a portion of the exclusion, depending on the circumstances that led you to sell. If your home sale was prompted due to job changes, illness, or unforeseen circumstances, you may qualify for a partial exclusion.

The percentage of the $500,000 or $250,000 gain exclusion that can be taken is equal to the portion of the two-year period that you used the home as a residence.

For example, say you as a single person bought a home for $600,000 in March 2023, lived in it for 15 months, and sold it in May of last year for $685,000 after moving out of state due to illness.

The maximum gain exclusion in this instance is $156,250 ($250,000 x (15/24)).

So, the $85,000 gain is fully excluded and tax-free. You can also use days or months for this calculation.

Death of a spouse and selling primary home

A spouse who sells the family home within two years after the death of the other spouse gets the full $500,000 exclusion that is generally available only to couples, provided the two-out-of-five-year use and ownership tests were met before death.

- There is also a welcome added tax benefit if you own the home jointly with your spouse.

- If you don't live in a community property state, **half of the home** will get a step-up in tax basis upon the death of the first-to-die spouse.

- The rule is more generous if the house is held as community property in a community property state. The **entire tax basis is stepped up to fair market value** when the first spouse dies.

Here's an example.

Let's say you and your spouse bought a home for $150,000 many years ago in a non-community property state, and it is worth $980,000 on the date that your spouse dies.

As the survivor, your tax basis in the home jumps to $565,000 (your half of the original $150,000 or <u>$75,000 basis</u> plus half of your deceased spouse's $980,000 or <u>$490,000</u> date-of-death stepped-up basis value).

Twenty months later, you as the surviving spouse sell your home for $1,100,000. Of the $535,000 gain from the home sale ($1,100,000 - $565,000), ***$500,000 is tax-free*** *and* ***$35,000 is taxed at long-term capital gains rates*** *that would be determined by where you would fall based on your tax bracket and marginal income tax rate.*

Home office deduction and selling a primary home

You may be wondering whether the capital gain tax on the sale of your home would differ if you took the home office tax deduction in prior years for using a room or other space in your residence exclusively and regularly for business or rental (e.g., as a home office or the rental of a spare bedroom).

It depends, but generally, the tax consequences are the same whether or not the home office deduction was previously claimed.

Gain on the office or rental portion generally qualifies as part of the $250,000/$500,000 capital gains tax exclusion for a primary home sale, subject to **two** exceptions.

1. **The first is for so-called unrecaptured Section 1250 gain, which applies "if you took depreciation deductions in the past" for the office or rental space. If you used the "simplified method" to claim home**

office deductions on your return, you don't have to worry about recapturing depreciation claimed in years prior to your home sale.

2. **The second exception applies if the workspace or rental space is in a building on the property separate from the main home—think first-floor storefront with an attached residence, rented apartment in a duplex, or working farm with a farmhouse or other unattached building on the property.**

Rental property and capital gains calculation

If you hold rental property, the gain or loss when you sell is generally characterized as a capital gain or loss. If the property was held for more than one year, it's a long-term capital gain or loss, and if held for one year or less, it's a short-term capital gain or loss.

The gain or loss is the difference between the amount realized on the sale and your tax basis in the property.

The capital gain will generally be taxed at 0%, 15%, or 20%, plus depreciation recapture at 25%, plus the 3.8% net investment income surtax for people with higher incomes.

However, a special rule that you must be aware of applies to gain on the sale of rental property for which you took "depreciation" deductions!

When depreciable real property held for more than one year is sold at a gain, the federal tax law requires that previously deducted depreciation be recaptured into income and taxed at a top rate of 25%.

This is known in the tax industry as unrecaptured **Section 1250 gain,** and the name is based on the number in the federal tax code section.

Sale of vacation home and capital gains

Gains from the sale of vacation homes don't qualify for the $250,000/$500,000 capital gains tax exclusion that applies to the sale of main homes. You will pay tax on the entire amount of your profit and if you are contemplating the sale of your vacation home, you must prepare in advance for the tax consequences.

When you sell a vacation home, your gain will be subject to the normal capital gains tax on real estate!

Therefore, if you've owned the vacation home for more than one year before you sell, the difference between your amount realized on the sale and your tax basis in your home is subject to capital gains tax rate of 0%, 15%, or 20%, depending on your income, plus the 3.8% net investment income surtax if you are in the upper-income tax brackets.

If you own the vacation home for a year or less, then any gain from the sale will be taxed at "ordinary income tax rates" up to 37%.

For example, say that in 2024, you sell a vacation home that you owned since 2010 for $875,000, and you have a tax basis of $635,000. Your $240,000 gain is taxed at long-term capital gains *rates. And just as you can't deduct a loss with your primary residence, so too is the case with your vacation property.*

What if you convert a vacation home to your primary residence, live there for at least two years, and then sell your home?

Can you qualify for the full $250,000/$500,000 capital gains tax exclusion?

Probably not, but it depends!

- If you sell a main home that you previously used as a vacation home, some or all the gain is ineligible for the home-sale exclusion.

- The portion of the gain that is taxed is based on the ratio of the period after 2008 that the home was used as a second residence or rented out to the total time that you as the seller owned the house.

- The remaining gain is eligible for the $250,000 or $500,000 home-sale exclusion.

Short sale of your main home and capital gains

After the great financial downfall in 2008, many financially distressed homeowners sold their home as a short sale in order to get from underwater mortgages on their home. If you are considering a short sale of your home, you want to know the tax consequences upfront.

A short sale occurs when your mortgage lender agrees to accept less than the outstanding balance on your loan to help facilitate a quick sale of the property.

The tax rules applicable to short sales differ depending on whether the debt is recourse or non-recourse!

Recourse debt is when the owner/debtor remains personally liable for any shortfall. If the lender forgives the remaining debt, a special tax rule provides that up to $750,000 in forgiven debt on a primary home is tax-free.

The owner/debtor will be taxed on any remaining forgiven debt at ordinary income tax rates up to 37%.

The tax results are different for **non-recourse debt**, meaning the owner/debtor isn't personally liable for the deficiency and in this case, the waived debt is included in the amount realized for calculating capital gain or loss on the short sale.

For primary homes, no loss is allowed, and up to $250,000 of gain ($500,000 for joint filers) can be excluded from income for homeowners that meet the ***two-out-of-five-year use and ownership*** *tests!*

These same rules apply if your home is foreclosed on.

Main Home Destruction and capital gains

If your principal residence is damaged or destroyed in a hurricane, tornado, widespread wildfire, or other federally declared disaster, you'll have gain to the extent the insurance proceeds you receive exceed your pre-disaster tax basis in the home.

Up to $250,000 ($500,000 for joint filers) of that gain is excluded from income if you meet the **two-out-of-five-year use and ownership** tests. If your gain exceeded those amounts, your gain over those excluded amounts would then be taxed at capital gain rates.

One way to delay the tax hit on all or part of the otherwise taxable capital gains is to use the proceeds you get from your insurance company to buy a new home within four years of the disaster. The so-called **"involuntary conversion"** rules are complex, so be sure to contact your tax adviser or other professional if you are thinking about this option.

Refinancing of your home or rental property and capital gains

As stated earlier and reiterated again, a refinance or tapping into your home equity are considered loans and no capital gains or any taxation on the proceeds will occur. Furthermore, if funds are used for home improvement, interest repayment may be deductible on your tax return annually.

Always keep in mind that with a refi you must have an effective repayment plan in place and there will normally be closing costs that can get into the thousands. You also want to ensure that your credit is at an acceptable level if you are seriously considering this option. A Home Equity Line/Loan may not have closing costs but will normally have a higher or variable loan rate.

If you failed to plan properly or not at all, a reverse mortgage is yet another option that you have if you find yourself in position where you need more income during your retirement years and you have a high equity position with your personal residence.

Section 1031 exchanges and capital gains tax

When real property used in a business or held for investment is exchanged for like-kind real property under Section 1031 of the tax code, all or part of the gain that would otherwise be triggered if the real estate was sold can be deferred. This tax break doesn't apply to main homes or vacation homes, but it can apply to rental real estate that you own.

The Section 1031 exchange rules are very complicated and difficult to navigate, with many requirements that must be met in a timely manner. Therefore, make sure to talk to your tax adviser and/or other professionals if you are seriously contemplating a like-kind swap of rental real estate that you own.

Opportunity Zone Funds and deferral of capital gains

The Qualified Opportunity Zone program was created under the 2017 tax reform law, the Tax Cuts and Jobs Act (TCJA).

- The program allows taxpayers to defer capital gains from the sale of business or personal property, including real estate, by investing the proceeds in entities called Qualified Opportunity Funds.

- These QOFs then use the money to help the development of struggling communities.

- As with many of the provisions in the TCJA, this program is set to expire after 2025.

Let's say you have a large capital gain from the sale of a rental home that you owned, and you want to defer paying federal income tax on that gain. If you can invest those gain proceeds in QOF, you could see meaningful tax benefits come your way.

The gains are deferred until the earlier of December 31, 2026, or when you dispose of your QOF interest.

The tax would generally be owed at that time on the deferred gains less the tax basis in the QOF investment!

The longer you hold a QOF investment, the more tax incentives there are. You, as an investor, would begin with a zero-tax basis.

If you hold your QOF investment for at least **5 years** your basis in the QOF increases by 10% of the originally deferred gain, meaning that **10%** of the deferred gain **can go permanently untaxed.** If you hold your QOF for at least **7 years**, your tax basis increases by another 5% bringing the total to 15%, meaning that **15%** of the deferred gain **can go permanently untaxed.**

If you ***hold your QOF investment for 10 years*** *you can increase your basis to fair market value, meaning that if you sell,* ***100%*** *of the deferred gain* ***can go permanently untaxed,*** *as no post-acquisition appreciation is taxed.*

Note: *the deferred gain from your real estate sales will be taxed in 2026 unless the updated legislation says otherwise.*

Time Limits

You have **180 days** from selling your real estate to invest the proceeds in a **QOF**. You can invest all your short-term or long-term capital gain proceeds from the sale or just part of the gains. However, if you invest part of the gains, only that portion of the gains contributed to the **QOF** qualifies for deferral.

If you decide to go the QOF route, "**you must elect" the tax deferral on your tax return for the year of the sale**. Be sure to follow the instructions on Form 8949 for electing deferral and reporting the deferred gain and be sure to submit Form 8949 with your return.

Also, you'll have to complete and attach Form 8997 to your return. **Form 8997** lets the IRS know of the **Q**ualified **O**pportunity **F**und investment and the amount of gain deferred, among other information.

Conclusion or Key Points

Whether art, antique vehicles, stocks, bonds, real estate, crypto or many other items that are sold for a gain—capital gains taxes may very well apply, and you want to know the likely amount that you will have to pay prior to the transaction (sale of assets) or before taxes will be due—not after.

When it comes to your personal finances, <u>whether you require a tune-up or major overhaul</u>, your awareness of capital gains at the <u>earliest time possible</u> will serve you well throughout your wealth building journey.

By having that awareness <u>you will put yourself in position to know what to expect tax wise</u> and you can plan for and take the amount that you will likely pay in taxes into the decision-making process and better determine if selling is your best option, or selling in a different manner, finding other ways to get the funds you need, doing a like-kind exchange when applicable or not selling at all—is your "best" option.

You can also reduce your capital gains after you transition by maximizing the gift tax guidelines while you are alive and participating in donor advised funds, (deduction can help reduce your overall taxes), charitable trusts and other estate planning options that can legally be done to reduce the size of your estate and increase what your heirs will receive and at the same time, reduce what they will have to pay tax wise after your transition.

Charitable trusts, including donor advised funds and others can provide tax benefits by reducing your taxable income, avoiding capital gains taxes, and removing assets from your estate. You normally need to have a sizable net worth and you will need a highly competent attorney who specializes in this area to educate and guide you in the process.

As a quick mental reference you can estimate roughly where you fall as far as "long-term capital gains taxes" are concerned if you know you will be selling assets that are assessed at the capital gains rate now or in the near future!

First determined whether you file as **S**ingle, **HOH** or **M**arried **F**iling **J**ointly and then commit the numbers below to memory and use those numbers as a "quick reference mental guide" to help you determine where you fall on the capital gains tax spectrum proactively—not reactively.

If you have income of roughly $50,000 or less and you are Single, you pay zero capital gains tax, the 15% rate falls roughly between $50,000 and $520,000 and anything over roughly $520,000 in MAGI (Modified Adjusted Gross Income) would be taxed at the 20% rate.

For **H**ead **O**f **H**ousehold tax filers, you can have an income up to roughly $60,000 and pay zero capital gains tax, the 15% rate falls roughly between $60,000 and $520,000 and the 20% rate applies for those who have MAGI above roughly $520,000.

For **M**arried **F**iling **J**ointly tax filers, you can roughly have MAGI income up to $100,000 and pay zero capital gains tax, the 15% rate falls roughly between $100,000 and $600,000 and the 20% rate applies to couples who have MAGI above roughly $600,000.

By committing the above numbers to memory (and realize that they adjust annually), you can use strategies to possibly pay zero in capital gains taxes and even when you have to pay, you will know or at a minimum have an idea of how the sale or cashing out of stocks, collectibles, mutual funds and other assets held outside of your retirement account will be affected based on capital gain rates, your income and length of holding of the asset.

Always keep depreciation recapture and the NIIT in mind—where applicable as they can get you into the "tax paying category" quite easily.

Also realize that <u>short-term capital gains are taxed at ordinary income tax rates</u> that apply, and further realize that income ranges used in the various tax brackets, along with **M**odified **A**djusted **G**ross **I**ncome amounts for long-term capital gains are adjusted annually, so the numbers will change.

However, **the above rough estimates** can be used as a guide to help you reduce or eliminate capital gain taxation and help you build wealth more efficiently at the various stages of your life.

In short, by analyzing your capital gains tax potential on the front end, you put yourself in a better position to make strategic decisions that can be of more benefit to you and your family in this economic climate—or any future economic climate—or even after you transition.

Also, if you are a high-income earner, be aware that an additional **3.8% NIIT** and/or the **AMT** may apply to your capital gains tax payment on your tax return.

Isn't it time you avoid short and long-term pain so that you can sincerely enjoy your capital gain!

You can now "fly high" as you pursue an unrelenting path toward capital gains and long-term wealth building success, as you have NOW been kicked out of your nest and you must now fly at an altitude that is your absolute best..

Chapter 7 Adjustments, Benefits, Credits & Deductions

Learn more about taxes and how you can save on your income taxes at this time...

It is important that you realize that there are ways that you can benefit from the tax code if you are a taxpayer in the United States and possibly its territories (and you file income taxes) that could mean more money in your pocket.

Even though you may be unable to use the large array of loopholes in the tax code that many millionaires and billionaires take advantage of, there are ways that you can benefit even if you have modest income.

In this chapter you will learn ways that you can possibly use adjustments, credits and deductions that can be of real benefit to yourself and your family so that you can build wealth more efficiently and achieve meaningful goals.

In the following paragraphs you will learn about adjustments that could possibly benefit you—along with credits and deductions that you can use to help make your desire to pay lower taxes, come true!

Adjustments

If you contribute to an IRA (and you qualify) and/or you are a teacher and you have teacher expenses that you pay out of pocket, you can adjust your earned income by claiming an "adjustment to your income" which would have the effect of lowering your taxes and possibly increasing your refund amount or reducing the amount of taxes that you would pay if you were in the unfortunate position of "owing" on your taxes.

As a taxpayer you can possibly subtract certain expenses, payments, contributions, fees, etcetera from your total income. The adjustments (Schedule 1 Part II) would be subtracted from total income on Form 1040 and would help you establish your adjusted gross income (AGI) that goes on page 1 of your 1040 tax return.

Common "adjustments to income" include such items as educator expenses, student loan interest, HSA contributions, alimony payments or contributions to a retirement account—among others, and you can possibly take these adjustments even if you don't "itemize" on your tax return.

Other Benefits You Must Know About

You must be able to tell if you can benefit more by claiming the standard deduction or the itemized deduction on page 1 of form 1040, and you must know whether it is best to use the standard mileage rate or the actual expenses (in order to switch from standard mileage to actual expenses, you must use standard mileage rate in year 1) when claiming the use of your vehicle for your business or farm—at a minimum.

Because all tax situations are unique, your tax professional may be able to clue you in on "other areas of your tax position that you are unaware of" to see where and if there are other areas in the tax code that you could possibly benefit from.

You may be able to contribute to your company retirement plan and get a pre-tax benefit as well as an employer match—and you definitely want to know about that so that you could contribute at a level that is best for not only your current tax position, but also at a level that allows you to meet or exceed your future goals so that you can do what you desire most during your retirement years.

If your income is at the right level, you may be able to qualify for a Retirement Savings Contributions Credit (a federal income tax credit designed to encourage low-and modest-income individuals to save more aggressively for retirement).

The credit equals 10% to 50% of your contributions for the year, up to certain limits and is based on your income qualification.

Credits

There are many tax credits that are available, and it is important that you (or your tax professional) know of the "tax credits that may apply to your situation" and how they could possibly be of benefit to you and your family at tax time or possibly benefit you and your family in future tax years.

To name a few, energy credits, earned income credit, child tax credit, other dependent credit, childcare credit, clean vehicle credit for electric car purchases, savers credit and home improvement credit, along with many others may be able to help you lower your taxes (technicalities must be met to qualify for many credits).

If you or your spouse are elderly and/or disabled you may be eligible for a credit, or if you anticipate future educational expenses for yourself, your child or your grand-child, there are ways that you can use educational savings accounts such as 529 plans among others, that provide tax advantages at the federal, state and possibly local level, if utilized appropriately. In future years (when you utilize funds to pay for qualified educational expenses for yourself, your children or your grand-children) you may be able to take advantage of the American Opportunity Credit or Lifetime Learning Credit so that you can reduce the amount of taxes you owe or increase the amount of your refund.

In addition, you (or your tax professional) want to be aware of what is possibly available at the state level as well, as in many cases "you will have to apply for the credit(s)" that are offered in a particular state.

Tax credits are more valuable than a tax deduction as you would have a dollar-for-dollar reduction (your tax credit would be $1,000 if you were eligible for a credit of $1,000 unless your taxes owed was below $1,000 and the credit was non-refundable, or you owed no taxes, and the credit was non-refundable) as opposed to the deduction being tied to your tax bracket.

If you are in the 22% tax bracket and you have a "$1,000 deduction" you would save $220—NOT $1,000 (.22 multiplied by $1,000) on your taxes when computing your tax deduction.

Deductions

You can choose between a standard deduction (2025 amounts provided by the IRS) or an itemized deduction (includes medical expenses, state income or sales taxes, property taxes, mortgage interest, charitable contributions etcetera, that you paid or contributed in 2025), depending on which one is most valuable to you from an overall perspective when you combine your federal and state taxes.

Deductions **are not as valuable** as a tax credit as a deduction will be based on your tax bracket and "is not" dollar for dollar!

To reiterate and further enhance your understanding, if you are in the 22% tax bracket and you have a $1,000 deduction you would save $220 (.22 multiplied by $1,000) on your taxes. On the other hand, if you had a $1,000 credit, you would save $1,000 on your taxes generally speaking—get the picture?

Conclusion or Key Points

It is important that you realize that "effective tax planning" is a "year-round process" and you need to know the importance of why you must be able to distinguish between a tax credit and a tax deduction as by having the ability to distinguish between the two, you can make better tax and wealth building decisions.

In addition, be aware of how you can use tax shelters such as starting a business, utilizing rental property or investing in a tax efficient manner (discussed in greater detail in chapter 9) to possibly lower your taxes. You want to assess and identify what you potentially can (or need to do) do to plan your tax moves in a proactive manner to better predict your future outcomes—thereby reducing your risk of owing on your taxes or having other surprises at tax time.

Always be aware that some tax credits are refundable, and some are not!

On the other hand, a tax deduction or an adjustment to your income can still be of value as it helps lower your taxable income, which means you're paying less in taxes overall. It can also increase your refund, but this depends on how big the deduction or adjustment is, what kind it is, your tax bracket, your income and your filing status.

A tax deduction (and/or adjustment) can only lower your taxable income and the tax rate (could potentially put you in a lower tax bracket thus saving you additional dollars that you would be paying if you remained in the higher tax bracket) that is used to calculate your tax!

This can result in a larger refund of your "tax withholding" on your **W-2, 1099-R, estimated tax payment(s)** or other documents in which taxes were withheld or paid.

A tax credit reduces your tax dollar-for-dollar, giving you a larger refund of your withholding, but certain tax credits can give you a refund even if you have no withholding (it is a refundable credit)!

Whether they go by adjustments, credits, deductions or any other name, the key point to remember is that <u>if they can be of benefit to you at tax time</u>—you want to know about them!

Even though you don't have to be a tax expert, you want to at least be aware of adjustments, credits, deductions and other ways of sheltering income that are outlined in the tax code <u>that can benefit you and your family</u> when you decide to file your taxes.

If you are a business owner or anticipate becoming one, be aware of the **QBI** (Qualified Business Income) deduction if you have a pass-through business with net income as the deduction can help further lower your taxes.

The tax code has a high number of adjustments, credits and deductions available, and if any apply to you or your family, you want to take advantage of them legally when you can do so.

All the best as you are now aware of the **ABCD test**, that you can use right now to analyze your taxes and make **a**djustments to **b**enefit yourself and your family. You are now fully aware of why you need to know about adjustments, **c**redits, and **d**eductions so that you can avoid financial destruction and build a foundation of wealth building that cannot be shaken—because the knowledge that you now possess—cannot be taken!

You are now in a better position to achieve at a level that is your absolute best, thereby ensuring that your finances won't be a mess as you achieve unlimited success, because you have decided to master the **ABCD test**—and put "the procrastination of your past" to rest.

Chapter 8 Understanding Compounding & the Various Types of Income

Learn how you can benefit from the use of compounding and understanding the various types of income...

Over the past several years we have had an increase in the number of questions regarding the topic of compounding, and in this chapter, we will address exactly what compounding is and how you can use the effects of compounding in your life to achieve the goals that will serve your and your family's best long-term interests.

What Exactly is Compounding?

First and foremost, it is important that you realize that interest is either:

1) Simple, or
2) Compound

SIMPLE INTEREST:

Simple Interest is a quick method of calculating the interest charge on a loan or the interest that will be earned on an investment.

Simple interest is determined by multiplying the interest rate by the principal—by the number of periods.

Simple interest is quite easy to understand as it is simply calculated as follows:

$1,000 at 7% interest is equal to $70 dollars in interest on an annual basis!

Over a 20-year period with simple interest you would accumulate ($70 times 20 years) $1,400!

Now let's look at COMPOUNDING...

Compound interest is when interest is added to the principal of a deposit, investment or loan, so that, from that moment on, **the interest that has been added** also earns interest.

Compound interest is often misunderstood by many, and it is calculated as follows (you need a financial calculator to compute):

$1,000 compounded annually at 7% for 20 years and you were to reinvest the interest, you would accumulate roughly $3,870—a difference of ($3,870 minus $1,400) $2,570 from the "simple interest" that you would receive over the same 20-year time period!

Now let's look at <u>$10,000</u> invested over a 20-year period at 7% interest using both SIMPLE and COMPOUND Interest!

$10,000 at 7% interest is equal to $700 dollars in interest with simple interest on an annual basis and over a 20-year period you would accumulate $14,000!

$10,000 compounded annually at 7% for 20 years and you were to reinvest the interest you would accumulate roughly $38,700—a difference of ($38,700 minus $14,000) $24,700 over a 20-year period!

Now you get the picture...

If the above returns were inside of your retirement account such as an IRA, 457, 403b, Thrift Savings Plan or 401k—no taxes would be due on an annual basis (you can have the following inside of your retirement account(s) among others): bank CD, Money Market Account, Bond Fund, Stocks, or Mutual Fund(s) etcetera.

If the above returns were outside of your retirement account such as in a bank CD, Money Market Account, Bond Fund, Stocks, or Mutual Fund etcetera, taxes would be due on an annual basis. Interest, dividends and capital gains would possibly be taxable.

Your emergency fund balance would be considered "outside of your retirement account" and the interest earned would be taxable on a yearly basis, however with savings and money market interest rates often low at times, the taxes would be very low. If the interest rates in accounts that you have "outside of your retirement accounts" rises or you have capital gains, you would be taxed on the interest or gain at your ordinary income or capital gains rate.

The key point to remember is that your money will grow at a faster rate if left untouched and the interest is compounded over time!

If you continue to add money to the investment over time your returns will be even larger over time!

Therefore, as part of your long-term strategy, you must come up with ways that you can invest both "inside and outside" of your retirement accounts at a level that will take you to where you need or want to be during your retirement years and beyond.

All of that sounds great you say—but where will I find the money to invest over a number of years, I barely have enough to live on?

You must first determine where you are financially by doing the following at a minimum:

1) You must have a system in place to determine your monthly cash flow so that you will know the amount of your discretionary income on a monthly basis.

2) You must put a plan in place to reduce or eliminate your outstanding debt (know money saving moves that you can make) and you may have to come up with a plan to get additional income and/or reduce your monthly expenses, or do a combination of the two.

3) You must properly establish an emergency fund.

4) You must <u>properly analyze and address all areas of your finances.</u>

If you can come up with a way to get just an additional $80 or so a month after or while you have addressed the above—after a 20-year period at 7% interest compounded monthly you could have over $40,000 in those account(s)!

If you could come up with a way to get an additional $800 per month—after 20 years at 7% interest compounded monthly you could have over $400,000 in the account(s).

If the investments were inside a <u>ROTH IRA</u> you would be able to withdraw the contributions tax free at any time—as taxes on the "contributions" have already been paid. If over 59 ½, you could withdraw the contributions and earnings tax free (certain restrictions apply) or let the account continue to grow as there are no mandatory withdrawals with a ROTH IRA.

If the contributions were made to a <u>Traditional IRA</u> you could deduct the contributions on your taxes on a yearly basis up to a limit (certain restrictions apply).

Once you withdrew the contributions and earnings during your retirement years you pay taxes (you would normally be in a lower tax bracket) after age 59 ½.

If you withdrew early (before age 59 ½) there would be taxes on withdrawal and a 10% early withdrawal penalty unless an exception was applicable.

If you have a family of 5 you could possibly save $80 or so on a monthly basis by going to coupons.com and smartsource.com and use coupons on items you normally buy and possibly save $80 or more per month.

You could possibly cut your energy costs by changing over to fluorescent light bulbs, installing an electronic setback thermostat, sealing air pockets in your home, sealing gaps in your home with insulation, cutting back on monthly entertainment, insulating your hot water pipes, reducing or cutting back on your internet/tv, ending monthly subscriptions—and by making any of those moves or taking any of those actions, you could possibly free up an additional $80 or so per month.

The opportunities for coming up with additional revenue are unlimited and you must use your imagination and your creativity to come up with more income or reduce your current monthly expenses on a consistent basis (or more likely, do a combination of the two)!

OK—Let's Recap...

Compounding is one of the simplest and least painful ways that you can utilize to help you reach your future goals in a more time efficient manner.

The key is to get yourself and your family in a "favorable financial position" by addressing your credit and finances in a critical manner on the front end or proactively.

Once you do that you can position yourself and your family properly so that you can invest in your future in a manner that can be of greater benefit!

Whether you are investing inside or outside of your retirement accounts you want to be in position to use the power of compounding to your and your family's best advantage.

Always realize that you may have to get additional income and/or cut your expenses to achieve your desired goals!

When you invest, you must be conscious of what is occurring! When an investment earns interest or dividends, your total amount invested increases.

That increased amount earns even more interest or compounds (if left alone) and the cycle continues if you don't pull out cash.

Be sure that you know the compounding frequency, the more frequent the compounding, the more you will earn!

Monthly compounding is better than quarterly! Daily compounding is better than monthly and so on!

If you invest on a continuous basis and/or increase the amount, the growth rate will be even more than if you did not do so!

Keep in mind that certain types of investments could lose value (stocks, bonds, mutual funds etcetera)—that is why it is important that you know how to invest in a manner that serves your and your family's best long-term interest (you must know the risk, time-horizon and other factors that may be unique to you and your family).

You must also realize that inflation will always raise its ugly head, therefore be sure to factor that in as your buying power will be negatively affected over time.

You can achieve untold success in your future and if you are truly determined, you will find a way to make compounding work for you and your family—not against (creditor's use of compounding to their benefit due to your unwise use of credit) you and your family!

It is important that you realize that credit card companies, consumer lending companies and other creditors use compounding to their benefit and to your detriment. Therefore if you currently have credit card or other outstanding debt, you must come up with a plan to reduce or eliminate that debt now!

Doing so at this time will put you and your family on a positive path to making compounding work for you, and will move you and your family in the direction where—success lives!

In addition to understanding how compound interest works, you must also have "Working Knowledge of the Various Types" of income.

Understanding the Various Types of Income

Over the years we have found that consumers are often confused by the different types of income that they hear or read about.

In the remainder of this chapter, you can put yourself in position to remove the confusion that you may have about the **various types of income** that you may hear or read about during the various phases of your life by comprehending the material at your highest level.

Active Income

Active Income is Earned Income. When you perform a service for payment in the form of salary, wages, commissions, or tips, you're earning "active" income.

Also, if you actively manage rental real estate, you will have "active income" that could be advantageous to you from a tax perspective.

Adjusted Gross Income

Adjusted Gross Income or **(AGI)** as it is often called is used in the United States (and other Countries) on individual income tax returns and it represents the total gross income that you earn for the year—minus certain deductions and is calculated on page 1 of IRS form 1040.

Taxable Income is adjusted gross income less allowances for adjustments, credits, exemptions and itemized deductions and **taxable income is the last entry on page 1** of IRS form 1040.

Taxable Income will be explained in greater detail later in this chapter.

For most consumers who file a U.S., individual tax return AGI is more relevant than gross income.

Gross income is income that you receive from all sources and includes sales price of goods or property, less cost of the property sold, plus other income.

Gross Income includes wages, interest, dividends, business income, rental income, and all other types of income that you may receive.

Contrast with **Adjusted Gross Income** which is income that you receive for the year—less deductions.

Several deductions (e.g. medical expenses and miscellaneous itemized deductions) are limited based on a percentage of AGI. Certain phase outs, including those of lower tax rates and itemized deductions, are based on levels of AGI.

Many states base state income tax on AGI with certain deductions, therefore you want to select a tax professional who understands this—and can use that understanding for your greater benefit.

After-Tax Income

The amount of money that you have left over after all federal, state and withholding taxes have been deducted from your taxable income equals your after-tax income.

After-tax income represents the amount of "disposable income" that you have to spend on future investments or on current consumption.

After-Tax Income is often called "income after taxes" or disposable income.

When analyzing or forecasting your personal cash flows (or budget and personal income statement), it is important to use an estimated after-tax net cash flow or your disposable income so that you can get a real feel of where you are financially.

This is a more appropriate measure because your after-tax cash flows are what you actually have available for consumption.

This is not to say that all of your investments are purchased with after tax income—some companies offer salary deferral retirement plans that deduct money on a pre-tax basis (401ks, Thrift Plans, 457, 403bs etcetera).

The money invested on a "pre-tax basis" would not be taxed immediately (benefit to you) but instead would be taxed once you decided to withdraw the funds (such as during your retirement years).

However, because most people have less income during their retirement years compared to their prime earning years, the amount of tax paid would normally be less.

Discretionary Income

Discretionary Income is the money that you would have remaining after all your bills are paid off on a monthly or yearly basis.

It is income after subtracting taxes and your normal expenses!

Your monthly expenses such as rent or mortgage, utilities, insurance, medical, transportation, property maintenance, child support, inflation, food and other miscellaneous monthly expenses that you pay to maintain a certain standard of living that you desire for yourself and your family would all be paid from your disposable income—and what would be left over is your discretionary income.

Discretionary Income is the amount of your income available for spending after the essentials (such as food, clothing, and shelter) have been taken care of on a monthly or annual basis.

To derive your discretionary income, you would take your gross income *and subtract* your taxes and necessities on a monthly or annual basis.

"Disposable Income" is often incorrectly used to denote discretionary income—therefore, it is important that you are able to distinguish between the two in your mind from the context in which it is spoken or written.

The meaning and your understanding of disposable income and discretionary income should be interpreted from the context in which it is spoken or written and not merely on what is communicated.

"Disposable Income" is the amount of **money you have left after the payment** of your "taxes" left to spend or save.

When applying for a loan (mortgage, consumer loan), lenders may take into consideration your discretionary income to assess your loan repayment capacity.

Discretionary Income provides the lender with more information on your capacity to repay than the debt-to-income ratio in the case where you have a lot of debt.

In some cases, potential borrowers may have a lot of income, such that the percentage of available income may be smaller than normal standards would allow, but the actual amount of money is still large and would support a loan that the borrower is requesting.

Always distinguish in your mind that "discretionary income" is the amount of your income that is left for spending, investing or saving **after** your "taxes and personal necessities" (such as food, shelter, and clothing) have been paid.

It is money that "you" have "discretion over" as to how you want to utilize it (spend or save)!

Discretionary income includes money spent on luxury items, vacations, savings and non-essential goods and services.

Discretionary Income is “derived from” disposable income, which equals gross income minus taxes.

The total discretionary income levels for an economy will fluctuate over time, typically in line with business cycle activity—and "discretionary income" on an individual or family basis will also fluctuate over time based on household income and expense changes.

When economic output is strong (as measured by GDP or other market indicators), discretionary income levels tend to be high as well.

Or another way of looking at it is when the economy is booming discretionary income will tend to be higher.

On an individual basis if you were to get a raise at your job, cut expenses or work a secondary job—your "discretionary income" would normally increase, unless you were deficit spending on a monthly basis.

If inflation occurs in the price of life's necessities, then your discretionary income will fall, assuming that your wages, your expenses and your taxes remain constant or relatively constant.

Discretionary spending is an important part of a healthy economy. People will only spend money on things like travel, movies, entertainment and consumer electronics if they have the funds to do so.

Some people will use credit cards to purchase discretionary goods, but increasing personal debt is not the same as having discretionary income.

And using credit unwisely can be a dangerous strategy as it is possible that you could run your credit balance up to a level where it would be difficult or impossible to repay in a manner that made good financial sense.

Disposable Income

It is important that you distinguish in your mind that Disposable Income is money that you have left after paying your taxes—while discretionary income is money that you have left over after paying your taxes “and” mortgage/rent, food, utilities, and life's other necessities.

Disposable Income is the amount of money that you and/or your household have available for spending and saving after income taxes have been accounted for.

Disposable Personal Income is often monitored as one of the many "key economic indicators" used to gauge the overall state of the economy, and it is calculated as follows:

Disposable Personal Income versus Discretionary Personal Income

If you earn $100,000 and were in the 28% tax bracket your "disposable income" would be $72,000 on an annual basis.

Let's say you have yearly household expenses of $40,000—your "discretionary income" would be $32,000 on an annual basis.

On a monthly basis your disposable and discretionary income would be as follows:

On a monthly basis your earnings would be $8,333 and your taxes would be $2,333, leaving you with a disposable income of $6,000.

With monthly expenses of $3,333 per month your discretionary income ($8,333 minus $2,333 minus $3,333) would be $2,667 monthly.

Be sure to understand the two examples above as by doing so you will be in position to understand disposable and discretionary income in clear terms!

NOTE: *State and possibly local taxes have not been taken into consideration in the above example.*

In 2005, the average **disposable personal income** dipped into negative territory for the first time since 1933.

This means that in 2005, Americans were spending their entire DPI or Disposable Personal Income—and then tapping into debt for further spending.

Do your best to avoid that scenario in your and your family's credit and financial life!

The disposable income per capita in the United States was over $60,000 according to many market watchers. Keep in mind the average number notably does not reflect the gap between the richest and the rest of society, as the gap is substantial.

Gross Income

Gross Income is your total personal income before taking taxes or deductions into account.

Your gross income is how much you make before taxes. Gross Income is the figure people are looking for when they ask you how much you gross a month or year.

Gross Income is an important number when analyzing your personal finances, it indicates how you could more effectively plan your and your family's credit and financial future.

Keep in mind that gross income varies widely from individual to individual.

You must always remember that "Gross Income" is all your income from taxable sources, before subtracting any adjustments, deductions or credits.

Be able to contrast that with Net Income which is your income after subtracting any adjustments, deductions or credits.

Investment or Portfolio Income

You must know that investment income includes income that you earn from savings and checking accounts, dividends from stock purchases and ETFs, Mutual Funds and other market investments that are in many cases taxable.

If inside of your retirement account or otherwise excepted from taxation the income would generally be taxable.

Modified Adjusted Gross Income

Certain tax calculations are based on modified versions of AGI.

The definition of Modified Adjusted Gross Income (MAGI) varies according to the purpose for which it is used.

These modified versions may add certain items to AGI that were excluded in computing gross income. Common additions include tax exempt interest and the excluded portion of Social Security benefits.

Modified Adjusted Gross Income or MAGI is often used when calculating the alternative minimum tax (AMT).

Net Income

Simply put, income is defined as money that comes into your personal household, usually generated as compensation in the form of a paycheck for work you and other household members have done.

Net income refers to take home pay, or the amount of money earned after payroll withholding such as state and federal income taxes, social security taxes, and pretax benefits like health insurance premiums.

If you are enrolled in a flexible spending account to pay for medical costs, the amount withheld from each check is also on a pre-tax basis.

Always realize that you save on your taxes when you pay for benefits on a pre-tax basis and if used effectively you can build a large nest egg that will allow you to enjoy retirement in a way that it was meant to be enjoyed.

If your employer matches your retirement contributions, be sure to contribute at least up to the match and even more if your financial position allows you to do so.

By doing the above you can put yourself in position to live your retirement in a manner that you desire—not in a manner that others desire that you live!

To maximize your retirement returns be sure to start early in your life stage and be sure to put a plan in place that allows you to reach your "retirement number" that you need to reach so that you can enjoy retirement on your terms!

In simple form Net Income is Gross Income *less* Deductions!

Net Income also includes other sources of income that you may have from rideshare driving, selling goods or services by doing a side job, getting paid for consulting services or selling products you've made or are reselling on eBay/Amazon, your own website, at art and craft shows or other venues.

Another form of income is passive income, which is generated when you rent out rooms, homes or apartments, or you earn capital gains, interest or dividends on investments or interest bearing accounts like savings accounts or some checking accounts.

Other types of income come from royalties, which are gained from agreements made relating to copyrights, patents, or gas, mineral or petroleum properties.

Believe it or not even bartering can be a way of generating income, if you strike a really good deal.

It is not uncommon for consumers to pursue multiple streams of income based on the times that we now live in.

If you are computer savvy you can track your personal finances on software, like Quicken or you can go online to mint.com or a vast array of new online players that have financial platforms.

Other helpful links that could help you improve your personal finances and income can be found by visiting TheWealthIncreaser.com website.

Ordinary Income

Ordinary income is income that is categorized for tax purposes as being taxed in the category that your income level falls based on your filing status.

Ordinary Income will vary from individual to individual and family to family based on the income that you earned during a tax year.

Ordinary income is any type of income earned by an organization or individual that is taxable at ordinary rates*, such as wages, salaries, tips, interest income from* bonds *and commissions.*

It is important that you contrast ordinary income with long-term capital gains, the rise in the value of investments owned for more than a year, and qualified dividends which are both taxed differently and are therefore not considered to be ordinary income and may receive a more favorable tax treatment depending on your income—so you must be aware of ordinary income and the role that it plays now, or the role that it could play in your future.

Ordinary Income comes in two forms:

1) business income and

2) personal income

In a corporate setting, the term refers to any type of income generated from regular day to day business operations, excluding any income earned from the sale of long-term capital assets, such as land or equipment.

Meanwhile, from a personal perspective, ordinary income can be defined as any sort of cash inflow that is subject to income tax, as outlined by the Internal Revenue Service (IRS).

In a nutshell "ordinary income" is any type of income that is taxable at ordinary rates—according to IRS guidelines.

Passive Income

If you were to collect income from a business venture in which you're not actively involved, you're passively earning income. This could include income from rental properties that you may own and investment returns.

There are tax advantages and disadvantages of having passive income and each taxpayer's situation will differ.

Personal Income

Personal income is also known as your "before-tax income" and is used in calculating your adjusted gross income for income-tax purposes.

Personal Income is basically your "Gross Income" that was discussed earlier. It is your total income before taxes or any deductions and can include various sources.

Tariffs

Although not a type of income, tariffs often cause an increase in prices for many products and can have a negative effect on your disposable and discretionary income.

In the spring of 2025 “tariffs” became a very popular topic around the world as tariff (trade) wars were created and many countries around the world were involved. Effective tariff policy requires serious study, analysis, foresight and planned negotiation—and if done appropriately can be an effective tool in managing trade more advantageously.

Tariffs are tax paid on imported goods by importers, and companies normally pass this and other taxes along to the consumer to maintain their profit margins and stay in business.

You want to know how tariffs will affect you and your family and plan accordingly.

Taxable Income

Taxable Income is a tax that governments impose on financial income generated by all entities or individuals within their jurisdiction.

By law, businesses and individuals generally must file an income tax return every year to determine whether they owe any taxes or are eligible for a tax refund.

Personal Taxable Income is derived by including all taxable income sources and subtracting out adjustments, exclusions, deductions and credits to determine your taxable income.

You must be able to distinguish between a tax credit and a tax deduction!

It is important that you realize that a tax "credit" reduces your tax dollar for dollar!

For example, if you owed $3,000 on your taxes and you were in the 25% tax bracket and you had a tax credit of $1,000—your taxes would then be reduced to $2,000!

A tax "deduction" would also reduce your taxes, however it would not be dollar for dollar—but would depend on your tax bracket!

For example, if you owed taxes of $3,000 and you were in the 25% tax bracket and you had a tax deduction of $1,000, your taxes would then be reduced to $2,750 (.25 times $1,000)!

The point is that a credit is more valuable to you than a tax deduction—so always keep that in mind!

You must properly purchase your home, and you must properly understand housing ratios!

Keeping your housing ratio under 30% and your housing and debt ratio under 40% of your monthly income are a wise use of benchmarks.

If your take home pay (or gross income) is $10,000 per month, your maximum mortgage payment should be $3,000.

$3,000/$10,000 = .30

or 30% on the front-end housing ratio (monthly housing payment only *versus* your monthly income)

If you have monthly recurring debt of 1 year or more such as monthly credit card debt of $500, monthly car payment of $500 and student loan debt of $1,000—your housing and debt ratio would be at 50% which in many cases would signify you had "too much" debt.

$5,000/$10,000 = .50

or 50% on the back-end housing ratio (monthly housing payment plus your monthly debt payments of 1 year or more *versus* your monthly income)

Keep in mind that compensating factors and extinuating circumstances (expected financial windfall, better school district for your kids—

etcetera) could make it possible for you to *have a need* to exceed the above benchmarks, however use caution!

In addition, you must ensure that your discretionary income (mentioned earlier in this chapter) is at an acceptable level so that you can live the lifestyle that you desire for yourself and your family.

If you were to eliminate your student loan debt of $1,000 per month prior to purchasing your home—using the above scenario your housing and debt ratio drops down to the more acceptable benchmark area of 40%—now you get the picture?

$4,000/$10,000 = .40 or

40% on the back-end housing ratio (monthly housing payment plus your monthly debt payments of 1 year or more *versus* your monthly income).

Income tax is a key source of funds that the government (local, state, federal) use to fund its activities and serve the public.

Most countries employ a **progressive income tax system** in which higher income earners pay a higher tax rate compared to their lower earning counterparts.

That is the case in the United States as well!

The first income tax imposed in America was during the War of 1812 and its original purpose was to fund the repayment of a $100 million debt that was incurred through war-related expenses.

After the war, the tax was repealed, but income tax in the United States became permanent during the early 1900's.

What it all Means in a Practical Sense

Understanding the various types of income that you may hear or read about from various sources daily or on occasion can be difficult to decipher if you do not have a mental system to distinguish effectively among the various types.

Below we will review what you have just learned to further increase your understanding.

• You now know that your Adjusted Gross Income represents the total gross income that you earn for the year minus certain deductions.

• You now know that your After-Tax Income represents the amount of money that you have left over after all federal, state and withholding taxes have been deducted from your taxable income.

After-Tax Income is the same as "disposable income" so be aware of the interchanging use of the terms.

• You now know that your Discretionary Income represents the money that you would have remaining after all your bills are paid off.

Discretionary Income is income after subtracting taxes and your normal expenses such as rent or mortgage, utilities, insurance, medical, transportation, property maintenance, child support, inflation, food and other miscellaneous monthly expenses that you pay to maintain a certain standard of living that you desire.

• You now know that Disposable Income *differs from* Discretionary Income.

It is important that you distinguish in your mind that Disposable income is money that you have left after paying your taxes—while discretionary income is money you have left over after paying your taxes “and” mortgage/rent, food, utilities, and life's other necessities.

Disposable Income is income that you have at your disposal "after" the payment of taxes!

Discretionary Income is money that you can spend or save at your discretion after the payment of your taxes "and" monthly expenses!

You now know that disposable income and after-tax income are basically the same thing—just expressed differently.

• You now know that your Gross Income is your total personal income before taking taxes or deductions into account.

• You now know that your gross income is how much you make before taxes. Gross Income is the figure people are looking for when they ask you how much you gross a month.

• You now know that your Modified-Adjusted Gross Income varies according to purpose and who is requesting that you modify.

All modified versions may add certain items to AGI that were excluded in computing gross income.

Common additions include tax exempt interest and the excluded portion of Social Security benefits. Modified-Adjusted Gross Income (MAGI) is often used when calculating the alternative minimum tax (AMT).

You now know that your Net Income refers to take home pay, or the amount of money earned after payroll withholding such as state and federal income taxes, social security taxes, and pretax benefits like health insurance premiums.

In short, gross income less certain deductions equal Net Income.

• You now know that your Personal Income is basically your "Gross Income" that was discussed earlier. It is your total income before taxes or any deductions and can include various sources.

• You now know that your Personal Taxable Income is derived by including all taxable income sources and subtracting out adjustments, exclusions, deductions and credits—to determine your taxable income.

Make it a point to increase your income and reduce your expenses so that you can enhance the future for yourself and your family!

You already know that you can increase your income by making compound interest work for you and not against you?

By understanding and being able to distinguish among the various types of income and understanding how compounding works, you put yourself in position to understand your personal finances in a more intelligent (meaningful and effective way that works to your benefit) manner!

You also put yourself and your mind in a more favorable position where you can control your future in a more "financially alert manner" and in a manner that will lead to true and lasting success for you and your family!

Chapter 9 Tax Strategies that You Can Use to Build Wealth More Efficiently

Learn how you can save on your personal taxes by using the tax code and strategic maneuvering to lower your taxes that you pay to the IRS and other taxing authorities…

In the current economy it is important that you use the personal income tax laws to your best advantage. Whether you are reading this book inside the tax season or outside of the tax season, you want to realize that tax planning is a year-round process. In this final chapter tax breaks and strategies will be presented, so that you can position yourself for more success throughout your lifetime.

In the following paragraphs you will learn what you can do to lighten your tax burden and possibly achieve your goals in a timelier manner if you are now a homeowner or you anticipate becoming a homeowner in the future!

If you are like most, focusing on your taxes is not a pleasant experience!

However, by focusing on and comprehending what lies ahead in your tax future you can possibly put yourself in a position to experience more pleasurable moments in your and your family's future.

Be sure to choose among the following strategies (if you see the benefit of doing so) and lighten your tax burden and achieve your future goals in a more efficient manner.

It is important that you find an approach to effectively manage your personal taxes in the current economy that works for you by providing ideas, concepts, knowledge and understanding that works with your mind—not against it. And it is important that you have some ideas—and knowledge about how you can lighten your tax burden so that you move toward your future goals in a more efficient manner.

Be sure to retain and utilize what you feel can help you achieve your dreams in a timely manner and run what you feel might work for you by your tax professional and others to see if any of the following tax strategies can benefit you and your family.

OK enough fluff—be sure to analyze how you can utilize the following strategies if you are now a homeowner or intend on becoming a homeowner in the future:

- **Mortgage Related Tax Breaks**

You can deduct mortgage interest, points, and your property taxes while you are a homeowner and have a mortgage and possibly property taxes even if you are not a mortgage holder.

You must "itemize your taxes" to claim deductions and by doing so you will save in taxes on your federal and state returns when applicable. In some cases, it may be to your benefit to itemize on your federal tax return even though you will get less back on your federal return by doing so.

The reason for doing so would be that you would get more on your state tax refund but less on your federal—but your overall total (overall tax refund of state and federal) would be more by itemizing. Many taxpayers take the quick way out and lose financially by not doing this analysis, thereby overlooking this potential option when it could possibly be to their benefit.

For example, if you will get $500 back on your federal taxes using the "standard deduction" as opposed to "itemizing" and $400 back in refund on your state tax refund using the "standard deduction" —your grand total is $900.

If you will get only $300 back on your federal taxes using the "itemized deduction" as opposed to utilizing the "standard deduction" and $800 back in refund on your state tax refund by itemizing—your grand total is $1,100.

Simple math tells you that you are better off electing to itemize—$1,100 minus $900 equals $200 more dollars in your pocket! It can be difficult to determine in many cases without actually "running the numbers" as state tax laws vary and all tax returns are unique. However, "electing to itemize" might be something that applies to your situation and there could be potential advantages (primarily more cash in your pocket) for you.

- **Improvements in your Home (Targeted)**

By purchasing solar panels, dual-paned windows, low flow plumbing, tank-less water heaters, doors, HVAC system and other energy improvements spelled out in the tax code you can possibly deduct them on your taxes if you itemize your deductions on form 1040.

Many home improvement energy related deductions often expire, and who knows what will happen in future years. However, at this time you can get a tax credit (applied directly against your taxes) of varying amounts during the tax filing season by taking advantage of energy credits that are available now, and possibly in future tax years.

- **Tax Exclusion from the Sale of Your Personal Residence**

It is important that you know that you can possibly exclude the sale of your personal residence from taxation if you utilized your home as your primary residence in 2 of the 5 previous years! If you are single you can exclude up to $250,000 of the gain and if filing as married filing jointly—$500,000 of the gain from the sale.

Therefore, <u>if you purchase right</u>—get a substantial appreciation in the price of your home and you decide that the time is right to move in a few years or so after the value of your home has appreciated—you could pocket a nice tax-free gain (be sure to run your plans by your tax advisor to ensure that you qualify).

Many savvy home sellers have used this approach, and although there is some risk that it is involved you can net a substantial **tax-free gain if** done successfully. If you are of the <u>personality type</u> that doesn't mind moving frequently, or you plan on moving frequently for other purposes—this could be a great strategy that could work for you.

Be sure to purchase in a neighborhood that has an upward trend in home appreciation using comparable sales data. Be sure that you know the risks and you have a properly funded emergency fund in place and little or no revolving debt so that you can reduce the risks involved for you and your family. Even so, there is no guarantee that after your home purchase the value of your home will appreciate as market dynamics can be unpredictable. Hopefully, you get the point, and you can clearly see the potential of how you could use this strategy to build wealth.

- **Cancellation of Debt**

Although not a pleasant use of the tax code or even an effective strategy for most (you probably lost your home) the "cancellation of debt provision in the tax code for mortgages" does lighten the sting of losing your home some as it could be even worse. If you are one who can use the **2007**

Mortgage Debt Forgiveness Act to reduce or eliminate your tax burden, you must do so.

The 2007 Mortgage Debt Forgiveness Act was extended through the 2016 tax year, and were further extended by Congress. If your mortgage debt was cancelled and the 2007 Mortgage Debt Forgiveness Act applies to your debt forgiveness you could legally avoid paying tax on the debt that was forgiven.

The federal Consolidated Appropriations Act of 2021 extended the Qualified Principal Residence Indebtedness (QPRI) exclusion through the year 2025.

Time limits apply for using this strategy so be sure you fall within the timeline of the act to take advantage of this strategy if you have received or anticipate receiving mortgage debt forgiveness in your future.

There is the possibility that forgiveness will be extended in future years.

- **Homeowner Exemptions at the Local, County & State Levels**

Did you know that many jurisdictions offer various "homeowner exemptions" that have the real effect of reducing or possibly eliminating your real estate taxes?

The exemptions vary from state to state—county to county—and in many cases city to city. However, they are available and it is <u>your responsibility</u> to search them out in your area and take full advantage of them.

Basic Homeowner Exemptions, Age Homeowner Exemptions, Military Homeowner Exemptions and many others are available. Again, it is up to you to find and enroll in them as they are in many cases not highly advertised.

Most have filing deadlines, so immediately after your home purchase be sure to inquire. If you used a real estate agent in the purchase of your home, your agent should be aware of the filing procedure in your area.

Key Points about Homeowner Tax Strategies

Be sure you are aware of what you can deduct or utilize in other ways (tax strategies) at the local, county, state and federal level. Be sure to take advantage of all homeowner exemptions that are allowed in your jurisdiction that you are entitled to.

All the strategies discussed in this chapter require that you own your property as an owner occupant (personal residence) and the strategies are not designed for rental or other non-owner-occupied properties.

You must always realize **that you have a unique tax filing position** and what may be effective and work for someone else, may not work for you!

For example, if your AGI (Adjusted Gross Income) is $70,000 and someone else's AGI is $40,000 and you go out and purchase $20,000 worth of solar panels and the person with $40,000 AGI does the same—you may be in position to utilize the credit either partially or in full, while the person with

$40,000 of income might not be able to utilize the credit at all.

This type of scenario can play out in many areas of the tax code—therefore effective planning with experienced tax professionals may be to your advantage.

Your income, family size, deductions, exemptions, education expenses, number of jobs, tax and other withholdings, tax payments etcetera are uniquely your own—therefore effective analysis must be performed.

Be sure to put into action your new found knowledge about the **Homeowner Tax Breaks & Strategies** that you can possibly take or make to ensure a more prosperous and productive future for yourself and your family.

As you move forward be sure to make a sincere effort to give it your best at all times. and use this chapter and book as a guide to empower your tax situation by analyzing your taxes in a more critical manner, whether you are now a homeowner or you anticipate becoming one in the future.

It is important that you proactively look at your tax situation (you must get out in front of your taxes) and not look back "for answers" after you have encountered a difficult situation or made bad choices. If you do not take the initiative to proactively attack your tax situation or any other area of your finances, you are making life on earth much more difficult than it should be for yourself and your family.

Don't be afraid to get planning advice on the front end (even if you have to pay as it can be money well spent) as most planners (at least those who operate at the top of their profession) are aware of strategies that you may not be aware of.

It is the hope that "Taxing Subject Matters Made Easy" has sparked something within you to make you look at your taxes and finances in a different way, so that you can start or continue on a serious path to achieving your dreams—starting today!

Escrow Accounts

Over the years there have been many questions about escrow accounts from homeowners and they all wanted a clear explanation of what escrow accounts were all about as it is rarely a subject that is explained in meaningful detail by many in the finance and real estate industry.

Let us first start by defining what a home escrow account is and then we can dive into some of the more frequently asked questions and answers that hopefully will put your mind at ease as it relates to homeowner escrow accounts.

A home escrow account is an account that homeowner(s) have that is established with their mortgage servicer for the payment of taxes and insurance—generally.

An escrow account acts as a savings account that is managed by your mortgage servicer. Your mortgage servicer will deposit a portion of each mortgage payment that you make on a monthly or otherwise agreed basis into your escrow account to cover your estimated real estate taxes and insurance premiums.

In a nutshell, it's just that simple!

Your escrow account will cover regular property taxes and homeowners insurance as well as flood insurance if it's required in your area. It does not generally cover water/sewer bills, storm water fees or other assessments by your local government. It does not cover homeowner association dues or supplemental tax bills.

It is important that you realize that your tax or insurance bill would be sent directly to your mortgage servicer, and you would normally not be involved in the process. In essence, you are relieved of paying those bills directly as long as you keep the account funded at the right level and you stay current on your mortgage loan.

If you don't have a mortgage on your home or you have a more exotic loan type, you would pay your taxes and insurance directly to your taxing authority and/or insurance company.

Also, once you meet a certain equity position (determined by your lender/servicer) you can elect to pay your taxes and insurance yourself!

Additionally, if you own your home outright you would not be mandated to carry insurance, however your tax payments would be mandatory, and it would be your responsibility to ensure that they were paid in a timely manner. It is also a good practice to carry insurance unless you can effectively "self-insure" your property.

Whether you need to have an escrow account or not will depend on your loan type and your lender. Government-backed loan options, like FHA and USDA loans, require an escrow account.

Lenders of conventional loans can decide if an escrow account is necessary!

Even if an escrow account isn't necessary, they can still be a good idea. If you don't use an escrow account, you'll be responsible for paying property taxes and insurance yourself, so you'll need to handle budgeting and paying them on time. You can simplify your "monthly finances" by setting up an escrow account if your mortgage servicer allows you to do so.

When you have an escrow account, your lender or mortgage servicer manages the payments and budgeting for you, and you'll be able to spread out your taxes and insurance payments over the year, instead of paying a lump sum all at once.

How Escrow Analysis Works

Your mortgage servicer and/or lender will estimate the amount that will have to be paid for your real estate tax and homeowners insurance bills. This estimate, provided during closing and often adjusted in future years, is based on the taxing authority and insurance company, or previous tax and insurance bills of the previous homeowner.

Each year, your mortgage servicer will analyze your account to make sure you're paying the right amount to maintain the minimum required balance according to a formula. Because the formula is based on an estimate of your taxes and insurance that can change over time, the amount can be overestimated or underestimated.

This is called an escrow shortage or escrow overage in the mortgage industry!

If there's an escrow overage, you'll get your money back with a refund—HOORAY!

If there's a shortage, you'll typically have a couple of options to pay the remainder—BOO!

Your first option is to pay the full shortage up front.

Another option would be to "pay the shortage over a period of 12 months" along with your regular payment. However, this option may not be allowed by some mortgage loan servicing companies.

You also may pay a "partial amount" with some servicers, and your payment would go up—but not as much as stated in the communications (Escrow Account Disclosure Statement) that you would receive from your servicer.

If you chose to "pay nothing" you would in essence be choosing to "pay the shortage over a period of 12 months" and your payment would go up by a certain amount—normally the amount stated in the communications (Escrow Account Disclosure Statement) that you would receive from your servicer a month or two before the escrow adjustment were to go into effect.

You would normally receive this notification 30 to 60 days before the monthly increase, thereby giving you additional time to decide which of the above options you would choose if allowed by your loan servicer.

How Escrow Works When Buying a Home

When you make an offer on a home, you'll typically include a personal check of 1-2% of the purchase price or other nominal amount depending on your state or jurisdiction. This is called "earnest money," and shows the seller of the home that you're a "serious buyer" and not merely wasting their time. The check will not be deposited until the seller accepts your offer.

If your offer is rejected, you'll get your money back, however if the offer is accepted, the money will go into an escrow account to be held until it's time to close.

Then, the money will be used toward your down payment and closing costs.

In this scenario, the escrow account acts as a **neutral place** for the money to sit until all paperwork is finished and the home is officially yours. Although this is an escrow account, it differs from the one held by your mortgage issuer discussed earlier as that escrow account is used primarily for property taxes and insurance of a home that has already been purchased.

Refund of Escrow

In cases where you overpay your taxes due to the servicer coming up with the wrong amount needed to pay taxes and it is over a certain amount, a refund check would be sent to you by the servicer. This often happens in the early years of your mortgage but could happen later depending on your particular area and circumstances.

If you have excess funds in your escrow account you would receive a refund check based on a formula. That refund check would in many cases be a welcome surprise to you.

Payment to Escrow

In some cases, you will have to make an additional payment in a lump sum or monthly to your mortgage servicer. If your taxes or insurance increased during the year or when your policy is renewed, you might face a situation where you would have to pay an additional amount to bring your escrow account back up to an acceptable level.

Other Costs Associated with Homeownership

In addition to your escrow payment that includes mortgage, interest, taxes and insurance there are other costs associated with home ownership that you must budget for on a monthly or annual basis and they include the following:

Special Assessments

In some subdivisions or neighborhoods, a "special assessment" could be put into effect for sidewalk or sewer improvements, and you would possibly be responsible for several years depending on the improvement, the amount and your jurisdiction.

HOA Fees

In some areas and communities, you may have to pay homeowner fees or association fees based on the amenities in the neighborhood.

Furthermore, many associations control what you can and can't do in the subdivision such as changing your house paint color, parking on the road, assessing penalties for your failure to pay HOA dues and other control mechanisms that seek to keep the property values as high as possible in the subdivision.

If you purchase your home in a subdivision with an HOA, be sure you ensure that the HOA is well managed and all dues are being collected effectively and the responsibilities of the HOA are being carried out consistently.

Utilities

You must account for utility payments such as water, electricity, gas, phone, internet, trash removal, and other monthly recurring costs associated with homeownership.

Stormwater Fees

In some community's storm fees are assessed to homeowners and they are often paid outside (paid separately) of your water payments and escrow payments.

Rapid Fire Q and A on Escrow Accounts

Q1: How does escrow accounts work?

A: Your escrow account allows your mortgage servicer to pay your real estate taxes and/or insurance premiums for you.

The payments are initially made by you to your servicer, and they subsequently forward the payment to the taxing authority and/or insurer.

Every time you make a monthly mortgage payment a portion is deposited in an "escrow account" that is managed by your servicer. An escrow account ensures that your bill is paid in full and on time and frees you from the task of handling those payments yourself.

Q2: Exactly what payments come out of my escrow account?

A: Your real estate taxes and/or insurance premiums. If you don't have a mortgage, you would not have an escrow account and you would pay your taxes and insurance directly!

Private Mortgage Insurance and/or Mortgage Insurance Premium (if you put less than 20

percent down at time of purchase) would also come out. Flood insurance and other fees if included on your real estate tax bill might also be included.

Q3: Where do I get the information that is needed to calculate my escrow payments?

A: Most loan servicer's will project your real estate and insurance payments based on past numbers, or information on your closing documents.

Q4: Can the amount that I pay monthly change?

A: Absolutely, it depends on the movement (up or down) of your taxes and insurance in most cases. With most servicing companies, a review is done at least annually and any changes (increases) in your mortgage payment will be reflected on your "Escrow Account Disclosure Statement" which you would receive after the review was conducted.

Q5: If I pay too much for the year, will I get a refund?

A: As mentioned earlier if you pay too much you will receive an escrow refund, and it would be a big surprise for you—prior to your reading of this book.

If you pay too little—you would have to pay a lump sum to possibly keep your payment the same or pay more on a monthly basis—again that too would be a big surprise to you, prior to reading this book.

Q6: How do I know if my payment calculation is accurate?

A: As to the accuracy of your payments, your mortgage company will perform calculations to ensure that there are sufficient funds. They would normally maintain a "minimum escrow balance" and under the law they may also add a small cushion in anticipation of changes in your

taxes or insurance premiums. Those amounts are added to your monthly mortgage, and you would pay them monthly.

If there was an overage of a certain dollar amount you would be refunded a portion. If there was a shortage you would owe an additional amount. You can do a ballpark estimate by dividing your most recent tax bill by 12. Your loan servicer will also have to keep a 2-month reserve in most cases.

Therefore, add two months to the estimate (i.e. $1,200 / 12 = $100 per month and $1,200 plus 2 months = $1,400--$1,400/12 = $117 per month estimate) and you will come up with a ballpark figure that you can use as a check.

Q7: Is a minimum balance required in my escrow account?

A: Yes, minimum account balances are governed by federal law or by your loan contract and applicable state law.

In most cases your minimum balance (excluding PMI or MIP) will be 2 months of escrow payments unless your loan contract specifies a lesser amount.

Q8: If my payment increases, can I still receive an overage check?

A: Yes, due to the most recent estimates for the year, you may receive a refund and when the taxes increase, the review by your servicer might signify an increase in your monthly payment "after" you have received your escrow refund check.

If you have an overage of $50 or more with many lenders and your loan is current, your loan servicer would be required to send you those funds rather than "decrease" your monthly payments.

Q9: Why can't my mortgage company apply the overage to future mortgage payments?

A: By law they must notify you if you have an overage of $50 or more and your loan is current, your servicer would be required to send you those funds rather than "decrease" your monthly payments.

If you desire to make an additional payment from the overage check you can do so, however you must cash in the check and indicate additional payment of principal or interest when you send in your monthly mortgage payment.

Q10: What options do I have if there is a shortage in my escrow account?

A: You can choose to pay the entire shortage (or in some cases a partial shortage depending on the lender) or pay the shortage over 12 months and that would increase your monthly payment.

If the additional payment amount will cause undue hardship, you can contact your lender and see what can be worked out. PMI or MIP may be able to be eliminated if your property and loan meets certain conditions and that would have the

effect of lowering your monthly payment. Other options such as loan modification may also be available. You also may need to obtain professional advice.

Q11: Are there penalties involved if I fail to pay my shortage in full?

A: No, if you elect not to pay for the shortage, your monthly payment will increase but there would be no penalties or additional interest payments due.

Q12: Why did my taxes and/or insurance go up?

A: Your taxing authority possibly increased the millage rate and/or your property value increased. Your home insurance policy may have increased for this same reason—among others. Based on projections made by your loan servicer your escrow account payment would then go up in most cases.

Q13: If I get news early that my taxes and/or insurance will go up, can I send in additional amounts?

A: You can normally send additional escrow account payments at any time, and your taxes and insurance would be paid. If there is an overage or shortage, your loan servicer would send you a refund or request additional funds or eventually increase your monthly payment.

Q14: If I pay monthly by automatic draft will my new payment amount be automatically adjusted because of escrow changes?

A: Yes, your mortgage servicer would normally adjust your payment based on the new payment. Please ensure that you have enough money in your account to meet the new monthly payment amount.

Q15: Will my third-party payment provider adjust my payment to meet the new payment amount?

A: If you use a third party, that can be a little trickier. You may want to contact them and let them know your new payment amount that was reflected in the Escrow Account Disclosure Statement.

Q16: Can I view my escrow account disclosure online?

A: Yes, most lenders have an online dashboard portal that allows you to do so. Many lenders will also mail you an Escrow Account Disclosure Statement notifying you when your payment will increase.

More on Escrow Accounts

Your escrow account allows your lender to pay your real estate taxes and/or insurance premiums for you.

Every time you make your monthly mortgage payment a portion is deposited into your escrow account and depending on when your taxes are due or your insurance policy renews—the money is pulled out and paid to the taxing entity(s) and insurance provider.

Whether your escrow was calculated effectively by your mortgage servicer and you are due a refund or if you may owe an additional amount, you can alleviate your fears by knowing how escrow accounts work on the front end—and planning for your future success.

You must timely know that taxes and insurance can rise or fall for varying reasons. You must know that the millage rates used to calculate your taxes are controlled locally and insurance premium increases are controlled by the company you choose, claim history, fire rating in your area, nearest fire department etcetera, and that too is your responsibility to timely know, when possible.

To alleviate your concerns about escrow account movement be sure that you establish a properly funded emergency fund and you have a conceptual overview of your life stages as that will benefit you greatly in your future.

Furthermore, you must know if you have a fixed mortgage rate or one that can potentially fluctuate.

Always consider the total cost of homeownership prior to your home purchase. That means you must know your mortgage payment including escrow, your utility payments, yard maintenance, age of HVAC, age of roof, water heater, electrical and other appliances and components of your home.

Your options will vary depending on type of loan and the fine print in the loan documents of your particular lender, when all is said and done.

You are now equipped with the homeowner escrow knowledge that you need to succeed.

You now know that when market downturns occur, such as the 2008 housing debacle, the economic downturn that we experienced due to COVID-19 or the trade wars of 2025 due to unnecessary tariffs, there is always a chance that your mill rate and taxes will remain steady or possibly go up or down due to market activity, depending on your home location.

You must also know that if you are in an improving neighborhood that is in high demand, your taxes could potentially go up!

It is your responsibility to plan on the front end for all scenarios whether an increase in taxes, insurance rates, special assessments, HOA fee increase etcetera—and it is important that you properly establish an emergency fund at the earliest time possible as you move along through the various stages of your life.

Tax Shelters

As tax filing seasons come, and go, many consumers have posed the question as to how they can more effectively shelter their income from taxation.

In the remainder of this chapter, we will discuss highly effective ways that you can shield your income from the tax bite. Be sure to comprehend and apply what you feel will work for you and your family, as by doing so you can keep more of your hard-earned cash in your and your family's hand!

Common Tax Shelters (for personal tax returns) include the following and will be discussed in detail.

- **Rental Properties (residential investment)**

- **Pass-Through Business Losses (sole proprietor, partnerships etc.)**

- **Tax Efficient Investing (stocks, bonds, mutual funds, ETF's, IRA's, 401k's, 403b's, 457's, thrift plans etc.)**

Rental Properties as Tax Shelter

Rental property income that you earn during the year can be offset against rental expenses and when you combine that with the depreciation deduction that you receive on an annual basis, you can actually end up with a loss that you can offset against your income for the year—thus lowering or possibly eliminating your taxes owed for the year—depending on your own unique tax position!

If you were Married Filing Jointly and you had:

Income of $120,000 less rental loss on tax return of $6,000 less itemized deduction of $40,000 less child dependent credit of $6,000 means that taxable income would be $68,000 instead of $74,000.

The rental loss of $6,000 has the effect of lowering the taxes for the individual listed above based on $120,000 of annual income. By effective tax planning, the individual listed above could (if they were in the right financial position) increase the number of rental properties owned and possibly bring their taxes down to zero.

Keep in mind that this is a simplistic example as other caveats may be present. After a number of years, they could choose to sell outright or by installment (depreciation recapture would normally apply and the gain would potentially be taxable at the capital gains rate that applied to their income level), refinance and pull money out tax free, do a 1031 exchange or continue renting out the property and earning rental income.

Business Losses as Tax Shelter

Another tax shelter that is available is that of a business loss from a sole proprietor or partnership that is taxed on the individual tax return. As a sole proprietor or partnership, you open a business and for the first few years of operations you might operate at a loss. That loss can be deducted on your personal tax return if you operate as a sole proprietor or partnership.

Using the same $120,000 of income listed above in this example, your taxes would be as follows:

Income of $120,000 less business loss on tax return of $12,000 less itemized deduction of $40,000 less child dependent credit of $6,000, means that your taxable income would be $62,000 instead of $74,000. In effect your taxable income was lowered by $12,000!

The business loss (keep in mind that you may have unlimited liability if you are a sole proprietor, therefore you must use this strategy with caution—you must know your business, the potential risks involved and decide if the risk is something that you are willing to live with based on the type of business that you have) of $12,000 has the effect of lowering the taxes for the individual listed above based on $120,000 of annual income.

By effective planning you could deduct the business loss on your taxes for the first few years of operations until the business started turning a decent profit, as your goal should always be to make a profit. Also realize you can turn trips that are personal/business into a deductible business expense if done appropriately.

Once the business was profitable, you could (if it made good financial sense to do so) go to a corporate type of ownership that would provide you with better liability protection and possibly a better tax structure and lower payment of taxes during your profitable years.

Tax Efficient Investing as Tax Shelter

Even though you can't eliminate all your investment related taxes, there are things that you control that can help you lower the taxes on your investment income!

You must ask yourself—how do taxes and annual fees that I have some control over affect my long-term investment horizon?

It is important that you realize that different types of investments are taxed differently depending on the type and whether they are held inside—or outside of—your retirement account!

It is important that you realize that the earnings from the following are taxed differently:

- **a taxable brokerage account that contains stocks, bonds, mutual funds, ETFs etc.**
- **tax-deferred accounts (i.e. retirement accounts) that contain stocks, bonds, mutual funds, IRA's, 401k's, 403b's, 457's, thrift plans, ETF's etc.**
- **a tax-free ROTH**
- **HSA or FSA Account(s)**

Also, it is important that you withdraw your funds from the above accounts in a manner that will minimize the taxes that you will pay!

Generally speaking during retirement, you want to withdraw from your taxable account(s) first (taxed at your ordinary income or capital gains rate) then your traditional IRA (mandatory withdrawals required at age 73 and taxed at the ordinary income tax rate—unless you had non-deductible contributions) and then your ROTH (no mandatory withdrawals required—particularly effective if you expect to be in the same or a higher tax bracket during your retirement years).

The key benefit of investing inside of your retirement account is the "tax-deferred compounding" that you will receive for a number of years (until you decide to withdraw—at which time the income will be taxed at your ordinary income tax rate).

For that reason, you must know the types of investments that are best suited inside or outside of your retirement accounts!

Be aware of index funds that invest in sectors, small companies, bonds, a particular country, or ETF's as they have the real potential to have a higher turnover than traditional index funds that are normally tax-efficient outside of your retirement account.

Other key tax moves are to consider holding periods, short versus long when you are selling your stocks, bonds or mutual funds held outside of your retirement account!

In addition, be sure to do your annual re-balancing on investments that are **held inside of your tax-advantaged retirement accounts** for the same reason as re-balancing inside of taxable accounts, to reduce your tax consequence—by avoiding or reducing taxation at ordinary income rate for short-term investments and taxation at the capital gains rate for long-term investments once you start withdrawing!

Those who fall into the lower income category can also shelter their income by contributing to a MyIRA, 401k or other retirement accounts and receive a **Retirement Saver's Tax Credit**. If married filing joint, you must earn less than $60,000—if head of household less than $45,000, and if single less than $30,000 (2025 tax year numbers—these amounts adjust annually)!

If you are eligible for the saver's credit and make the proper contributions, you could receive a tax credit up to $2,000 if Married Filing Joint and lower amounts if Head of Household or Single.

As a credit it would reduce your taxes dollar for dollar, but the credit is not refundable, meaning the credit could only take your taxes to zero.

If you are a business owner you may be able to hire your children (be sure they are performing actual duties based on market wages for the type of job that they do) and **pay them up to the amount of the standard deduction for single filers** and they **would not** be "required" to file a tax return and you could deduct their wages or salary from the gross income of your business.

Furthermore, your children could establish an IRA, either ROTH or Traditional or a combination—and your children could begin on a journey of funding their retirement account at an early age—or possibly even use the account in the future for a home purchase or educational purposes (tax free if they meet the technicalities in effect during that tax year).

Even as an IRA holder yourself, you can use the proceeds for yourself, your child or grandchild for educational purposes or purchase of their first home, and that could be effective if used appropriately. If you are in position to set up an IRA and you have reached “your retirement number” outside of your IRA account(s), or are on target to do so, it could be an effective strategy (technicalities apply).

Additionally, you want to consider education planning as early as possible as **529 and other tax advantage plans** can incur earnings that are tax free if used for educational purposes. In some states you can even get a tax credit or deduction on your state income taxes when you file.

You must at this time desire to get started on a serious path to success and you can now do so by choosing effective tax strategies and having a real yearning to give it your best as you journey toward success!

Key Points on Tax Shelters

You must always realize that tax-time is only the beginning when it comes to your tax planning!

You must consider the annual effect of your income, your expenses, your tax position, your net worth and what you can do to reduce or eliminate the taxes that you may owe!

The Common Tax Shelters mentioned in this chapter are proven ways that taxpayers have reduced their tax burden for years, and you can do the same.

Be sure you hire competent professionals who can help you attain your future goals legally—but with a lower tax bill as the ultimate outcome. You must have a desire to minimize your and your family's taxes in the future.

You must "actively engage your mind" to find ways that you can lower your annual taxes!

Be sure to utilize the capital gains strategies mentioned in chapter 5 and other strategies that you have learned throughout this book to further maximize your tax savings.

Always realize that the higher your income, the more you can benefit from tax-shelters—generally speaking.

*With the top tax rate now at **37% on ordinary income** and **20% on qualified dividends**—tax shelters are more important than ever.*

Keep in mind that the higher your income, the more potential tax shelters that you also have at your disposal.

If you are a high earner, you may also have to pay a 3.8% NIIT surtax on certain investment income, so use tax shelters appropriately based on your own unique situation.

When you consider utilizing any of the tax shelters mentioned in this chapter, you must realize that your personal situation will be the key to selecting an approach that will work best for you and your family.

All the best to your tax strategies and lasting wealth building success...

GDP & The Broader Economy

It is important that you analyze market indicators and particularly the GDP while analyzing your taxes and investing in your future.

Gross Domestic Product (GDP) is the total monetary value of all final goods and services produced within a country during a specific time period, typically one year. It is commonly used to measure the economic performance and health of a country.

GDP, National Debt, Market Indicators and Major Indexes may clue you in on where economic activity is headed—therefore be aware of economic indicators and have your antennae up for what may come to you inspirationally **that can direct you** towards what you need to do.

As the stock market and major indices such as the S & P 500, Nasdaq, RUSSELL, and others continue to fall or rise—you no longer have to use your approach as a disguise!

Is the market expanding or retracting?

What does your intuition tell you about what is happening around you—and what is happening in the larger economy?

Are you one who lets anxiety overrule you when you see negative news about the GDP, and the national debt?

As important as you may think your concerns are, it is more important that you focus on "what you can do proactively" as opposed to focusing on that which you can't change—or won't change!

Conclusion or Key Points

Your ability to look at your tax position proactively is one of the most critical moves that you can make early in your life stage, or at the earliest possible time during your life if you are one who sincerely desires to attain tax and wealth building success efficiently.

You want to know the **basics of taxation** and possible **advantageous moves that you can make** throughout your lifetime.

Depending on your unique circumstances, there are many potential tax strategies that you can use to reduce or eliminate your taxes and **Taxing Subject Matters Made Easy** has presented numerous potential options that may work for you and your family, however many more may potentially exist for you, as all tax filing situations are unique.

You also want to keep in mind the current state of political, regulatory, economic, social, technological and legal happenings in your country and throughout the world, as risk levels have increased, and what was once thought to be a foregone conclusion in the building of wealth, may now need to be given a second thought at a deeper level of intensity.

As a result of reading **"Taxing Subject Matters Made Easy"** you are now in a better position to look at and respond to tax issues in your and your family's life, and you are now better equipped to ask the right questions when you communicate with tax and other professionals as it relates to your financial future.

Even though new tariffs have triggered market volatility and talk of recession at the time of the publishing of **Taxing Subject Matters Made Easy**, along with retaliatory tariffs from many countries that were once major U.S. trading partners, you want to position yourself for greater success by obtaining the right knowledge proactively so that you can better control your taxes and financial future.

In the **appendices and bonus section**, you will be introduced to a **3-step financial management approach** and an **investment simplification approach** that can consolidate your knowledge and insight and put you in position to better handle the tariff turbulence and other market activity so that you can stay focused on your short, intermediate and long-term goals and move forward with confidence in the current economy, or any economy.

Always be aware of changing market activity as you may have to adjust along the way as the situation (market volatility at any given time from various causes) evolves.

Additionally, you want to file your taxes (or file for an extension) in a timely manner as **tax compliance** is in many cases as important as **sheltering your income** from taxation. Always remember that your failure to file or failure to file and pay in a timely manner can result in penalties, and in some cases criminal prosecution.

Late filing can incur penalties of .05 per month and failure to file penalties can be as high as 25% total. A minimum failure to file penalty may also apply depending on your circumstances. If both apply, after 5 months the failure to file penalty will max out, but the failure to pay penalty continues.

By utilizing what you have learned in this book along with "strategic tax planning" you can now achieve more, and you should now feel much better equipped and worthy of attaining lasting success throughout your lifetime.

Appendix A

Other books by Thomas (TJ) Underwood

Book 1) Managing & Improving Your Credit & Finances for this MILLENNIUM©2012

Book 2) HOME BUYER 411 *The Smart Guide to Buying Your Home*©2014, updated 2023

Book 3) HOME SELLER 411 *The Smart Guide to Selling Your Home*©2014, updated 2023

Book 4) The Wealth Increaser©2014, updated 2023

Book 5) The FIZBO Manual©2014, updated 2023

Book 6) 1-2-3 Credit & Me©2021, updated 2023

Book 7) The 3 Step Structured Approach to Managing Your Credit & Finances ©2014, updated ©2023—amazon release in June

Book 8) Credit & Finance Improvement Made Easy ©2014, 2023—amazon release in August

Book 9) Wealth Building AXIOMS Volume 1©2024

Book 10) Wealth Building Now ©2024—amazon release in April

Book 11) Taxing Subject Matters Made Easy ©2025—amazon release in May

Thomas (TJ) Underwood has created over 700 pages of credit, finance, and wealth building articles covering the entire spectrum of personal finance on three websites. He is also the Author of over 10 books that are part of **The Real Estate & Finance 360 Degrees Series of Books©** that are designed **to help consumers achieve success in an intelligent, consistent and proactive** manner.

He considers it an honor to use his rare combination of experience as a former fee-only financial planner, former top-producing loan processor and current position as an active real estate broker serving the Atlanta Metropolitan area to provide readers enlightening personal finance systems and approaches that they can implement in their life that will provide them the opportunity to achieve what they truly desire in the most efficient and effective manner possible.

The creation of numerous books over the past 15 years has brought forth a new version of financial planning that turns the odds in your favor (not creditors) and more importantly puts you in control of your finances and wealth building activity in a way that could lead to greater success for you and your family throughout your lifetime.

In the **preceding chapters,** you have learned about "tax knowledge" that can transform your life if applied appropriately, and the material can help you achieve your tax, financial (and life) goals at a higher level "in this and the coming decades" while you are here on planet earth.

Be sure to visit the following sites to enhance your tax and wealth building knowledge and achieve even more throughout your lifetime:

TheWealthIncreaser.com

Realty-1-Strategic-Advisors.com

The-best-atlanta-real-estate-advice.com

Appendix B

The 3 Step Structured Approach (A Comprehensive Financial Management System)

In easy-to-understand format, you must know how to:

1) Utilize personal finance statements appropriately

1. Establish a personal **b**udget or cash flow statement at a minimum
2. Create a personal **i**ncome statement
3. Create a personal **b**alance sheet
4. Create a personal **n**et worth statement

2) Gain mastery of how you manage your credit

Negative information must be kept off of your credit report

Utilization of your available credit must be at a reasonable level

Time of open accounts is important

Types of accounts are important

Inquiries must be kept at a reasonable level

3) Comprehensively understand your finances in the following areas

Insurance

Investments

Taxes

Emergency fund

Education planning

Estate Planning/Wills

Retirement planning

By just being **exposed to** the **3 steps** above--you are far ahead of the average consumer who for the most part has no real understanding of what personal finance encompasses—let alone the ability to use the knowledge of what personal finance encompasses to their and their family's greater benefit.

What you need to do financially

Now that you have knowledge of what you need to know (pun intended) **you must take the right steps** and put into action the results of your cash flow statement or budget at a minimum. Whether you have a monthly surplus or a monthly deficit you are now in position for more effective planning from this point forward.

If you are comfortable with numbers, you may also want to create an income statement and balance sheet so that you can determine your net worth at this time—and improve upon your net worth in the coming years.

The creation of a "properly funded emergency fund" will go a long way in helping you increase your net worth in future years!

You must also gain mastery over how you manage your credit by knowing how to **utilize your knowledge of the 5 credit factors**—as that knowledge can prevent you from getting into a difficult financial hole where climbing out is difficult or highly unlikely (you may need to consider filing bankruptcy as a real option).

Finally, you must know how to select the appropriate insurance products and investment options along with doing, education planning, estate planning and retirement planning in a manner that is more advantageous for you and your family—not creditors or others who have no real concern for your lasting success.

The importance of reviewing what you do financially

Now that you have a comprehensive overview of your finances and you have been **exposed** to all that you need to know (and do) to work toward making your wealth building goals come true, you "must" be aware of your need to review!

You must review your personal finance statements, including your emergency fund to make sure you are adequately protected. You must review your understanding of the 5 credit factors so that you can make the right or at a minimum, good decisions as it relates to your use of credit.

You must review your insurance, investments, taxes, education planning, estate planning/wills, and retirement planning on a routine basis to see where improvements can be made.

Regardless of your past experiences, the environment in which you grew up in and the positive or negative exposures in your life, you are now in position to change all of that to your advantage—and by being **exposed to personal finance** in a way that you can readily understand and utilize, you are now ready to take your prize.

It is important that you are **exposed to all areas of financial planning** that you need to do throughout your life at the earliest possible time. By doing so you can get out in front of potential disruptions and "proactively plan your future" in a manner that is more advantageous for you and your family.

You can put yourself in position where you can live with confidence and the success that you desire will not only occur—it will be expected. You no longer need to approach your financial future with doubt, uncertainty, and a feeling of "can't do"—as by purchasing this book you have positioned yourself in a major way to make your dreams come true.

All the best because of your willingness to be "exposed to financial systems" that can lead to lasting success.

The 3 Step Structured Approach to Improving Your Credit & Finances®

Step 1

BIB N

You can easily remember BIB N

B—stands for Budgeting or Cash Flow Statement

I—stands for Income Statement

B—stands for Balance Sheet

N—stands for Net Worth Statement

The above statements are all personal finance statements, and you will need to create and analyze each one. Be sure to be as accurate as possible with the data you enter.

Once analyzed, you will have to determine ways that you can improve each statement and then come up with a written plan of action for improving each statement so that your financial ratios and net worth will move in the right direction.

Step 2

Remember **NUTTI** or **MUTTI** in your GUTTI to improve your credit score forevermore.

This too, you can also easily remember:

N stands for Negative Information—**M** is for Messed Up—if either occur, your credit will be highly affected as this generally makes up 35% of your credit score.

U stands for Utilization or how you use your credit, and it too is very important as this generally makes up to 30% of your credit score.

T stands for Time and is another important factor as you should keep older accounts open and always pay on time. Just as "i" in time comes before "y" in type, time comes before type when you are memorizing this acronym. Time generally makes up to 15% of your credit score.

T stands for Type and it comes after time. The types of credit you have are important as a good mix is better than no mix. If you have several credit cards, a home loan, and an auto loan that would be a better type of credit than just having several credit cards. The type of credit makes up to 10% of your credit score.

I stands for Inquiries and you should keep your inquiries low if you will be seeking new credit and/or are attempting to improve your credit score. Inquiries also make up to 10% of your credit score.

Note the descending order of the percentages above are:

N or **M** = 35%

U = 30%

T = 15%

T = 10%

I = 10%

Total 100%

Remembering in that order will also help structure the acronym so keep the percentages along with what each acronym represents fresh in your mind.

If your credit is unsatisfactory at this stage, you will have to clean up your credit and work on getting your credit position to an acceptable level so that you can reach your future goals and objectives.

Step 3

My Eyes Tear

My Eyes Tear when I see that my financial future is clear.

The above sentence is a play on words and the memory triggering aspect is:

Your eyes would represent the (**ii's**).

Your tear would represent the (**teeer**) in the following acronym.

The first (**I**) represents your Insurance Planning

The second (**I**) represents your Investment Planning

The (**T**) represents your Tax Planning

The first (**E**) represents your Emergency Fund

The second (**E**) represents your Education Planning

The third (**E**) represents your Estate Planning/Wills

The (**R**) represents your Retirement Planning

You will have to analyze each area of your finances and see what you need to do immediately and, in your future, to improve your position. You should also know at this point what you will need to do in the future as you may not be in financial position now to address all of your financial concerns.

However, you should be aware at this stage of what you need to do in “all areas” of your finances.

Now, do you think you can cultivate a mental framework or mindset that includes the **3 steps above**? Of course you can!

OK, Let’s Review

- **BIB N** stands for...

- Remember **NUTTI or MUTTI** in your GUTTI to improve your credit score forevermore and each letter in **NUTTI and MUTTI** stand for...and the percentage in each letter stand for...

- **My EYES TEAR** when I realize my financial future is clear and **your eyes are your (ii’s)** and **your tear are your (teeer)** and each letter stands for...

Recite it in your mind until all of the “3 Steps” become second nature to you. Don’t get too concerned about the deeper understanding of each letter at this time as they will come to you if you navigate www.realty-1-strategic-advisors.com and/or you purchase **Managing & Improving Your Credit & Finances for this MILLENNIUM**—our new book.

It will all come together for you by navigating **TheWealthIncreaser.com**—our most recent blog site.

With just what you have just learned you put yourself ahead of most consumers when it comes to the effective understanding of personal finance.

This is only the beginning of your journey to financial freedom. Just mastering and understanding the 3 steps listed above are well worth the price you paid for this book as you now have the essentials of what you can do in your future to attain lasting success.

Open your mind, ears, and eyes wide as we go into deeper detail of how you utilize **The "3 Step Approach" to Managing & Improving Your Credit & Finances** in your and your family's life—today!

Get your "mindset" to the point where for the rest of your life you will always know:

BIB N—Remember **NUTTI or MUTTI** in your GUTTI to improve your credit score forever more—and my **EYES TEAR** when I realize my financial future is clear.

Once you have the above acronyms solidly memorized you will be well on your way to living your life in a manner that suits you and your family best—not your creditors.

Be sure to comprehend the above acronyms at your highest level. In other words, open your mind, ears, and eyes wide and put on your thinking cap.

In this short appendix you have the opportunity to master your understanding of credit and finance in a style and manner rarely seen—in personal finance.

This book was intentionally written in a somewhat entertaining and engaging style with serious content that was designed to get your mind to open up.

By reading this short book you should be in great position to apply the information and change your and your family's financial condition for generations.

Final Thoughts on The 3 Step Structured Approach

It is critical that you have the proper understanding, and you know how to properly apply the helpful acronyms that you have learned.

You must at all times know:

1)

that you need to properly create and analyze your **B**udget or Cash Flow—so that you know your inflow and outflow of cash on a monthly basis.

Even if you decide to create an **I**ncome Statement, **B**alance Sheet Statement and **N**et Worth Statement later—you need to create at a minimum a Budget or Cash flow Statement—at this time!

2)

Your understanding and application of Remember **NUTTI** or **MUTTI** in your GUTTI to improve your credit score forevermore.

Improving Your Credit Score in a Nutshell

Remember **NUTTI or MUTTI** in your GUTTI to maximize your credit SCORE, FOREVERMORE!

Follow me here...It will make sense...I promise...

N---"Negativity"---try to avoid negative information in your payment history---35% of your score

U---keep "Utilization" and amount owed low---keep debt low---30% of your score

T---always pay on "Time," keep old accounts open---15% of your score

T---keep a good mix and have different "Types" of credit---10% of your score

I---keep "Inquiries" low by loan shopping within a small window---10% of your score

Or Another Way to Look At It

M---don't "Mess up" your credit---try to avoid "negative info" on your report---35%

U---keep "Utilization" at a low percentage of your total debt---keep debt low---30% of your score

T---always pay on "Time," keep old accounts open---15% of your score

T---keep a good mix and "Type" of credit---10% of your score

I---keep "Inquiries" for the last 12 months low if you will be seeking new credit---10% of your score

Did you know that I set you up for a short catchy Acronym (although somewhat strange) that has the potential to help you take control of your credit for the rest of your life?

If you memorize and utilize the following phrase in the right manner, you will be in position to improve your credit position. Feel free to pass it along to your family and friends to help them improve their credit score and credit situation as well.

Although the Acronym (memory trigger) is somewhat "weird" you should easily remember it for the rest of your life by reciting it in your mind on a constant basis—until you are confident that you have it memorized, and you understand the underlying concepts behind the acronym.

Remember NUTTI or MUTTI in your GUTTI to maximize your credit SCORE, FOREVERMORE!

By simply memorizing the preceding Acronym and utilizing the knowledge gained—you can take positive control of your financial situation—and that of your loved ones. OK—one last time…

N stands for ... and M stands for... 35% of your score

U stands for... and U stands for...30% of your score

T stands for... and T stands for...15% of your score

T stands for... and T stands for...10% of your score

I stands for... and I stands for...10% of your score

OK, your time is up, I'm sure you have all the factors that go into maintaining and improving your credit and credit score mastered.

It is also important that you realize that there are two major scoring models:

1) **FICO score**
2) **VantageScore**

If you utilize the five factors above appropriately, you will have a good to excellent credit score regardless of the model that is being used. Always realize that newer models, older models, industry specific models and other models are on the market at the same time and the calculation of your scores will vary depending on the model used by the creditor or the entity requesting your score!

Furthermore, you should know that there are 3 major credit bureaus:

1) **TransUnion**
2) **Equifax**
3) **Experiean**

An easy way to remember the 3 major credit bureaus is to think that you will be TEEing off—however it won't be for golf—

but for improving your credit and credit score!

The above structuring technique brings clarity to help you improve and maintain you credit for the rest of your life. By simply remembering the weird poem or statement—you put yourself in a position to always know what you need to do to improve and maintain your credit.

It is also important that you realize that consumers who must be concerned about the FCRA (Fair Credit Reporting Act) and other corrective credit improvement systems—normally are those who have mismanaged their credit in the past.

It is imperative that you manage and improve your credit and finances in a **more intelligent, consistent, and proactive manner**—in order to avoid getting into a credit position that is adverse for you and your family!

You can choose to learn other creative ways or even learn the FCRA standards and guidelines and other systems of credit and finance management if you choose too—however we do not believe you will find a more effective and efficient system than "Remember **NUTTI or MUTTI** in your GUTTI to improve your credit score forevermore"—that you have learned in this precise and to the point guide.

However, do not use our beliefs **as an excuse** to not do your due diligence and determine for yourself if there is a better system or approach that is available that will work better for you and your family.

It is imperative that you use your intelligence to analyze other credit and finance systems in an **analytical, accurate, careful and critical manner** and decide for yourself what works best for you and your family!

If you comprehend and master the use of "Remember **NUTTI or MUTTI** in your GUTTI to improve your credit score forevermore"—you will primarily have what you need—to succeed when it comes to managing and improving your credit for the rest of your life.

It is important that you realize that the **"3 Step Approach"** and the Credit Improvement system mentioned above will essentially provide you with what you need once you get your credit properly established.

If you desire a comprehensive system that can move you forward on a continuous basis—you have found that with the "3 Step Approach."

Therefore, don't get too uptight or concerned about your credit as long as you have a thorough understanding, and you know how to apply in a practical manner (and you actually do so)—"Remember **NUTTI or MUTTI** in your GUTTI to improve your credit score forevermore."

Be sure you understand and remember the **ratio percentages** for each letter as by doing so you will be well ahead of 90% of the population when it comes to the understanding and application of credit. And having the ability to maintain and increase your credit score on a consistent basis is an important skill set that you can pass along to others.

Be sure that you understand that different jargon may be spoken or written regarding the credit factors mentioned above, and it is your responsibility to understand that jargon.

By mastering the **"3 Step Approach"** you will even have a more effective and efficient practical system of credit and finance management and understanding than many professionals who work in the financial industry.

You can choose to waste or perhaps not waste your time by learning about the FCRA (Fair Credit Reporting Act), CFPB (Consumer Finance Protection Bureau), USA.gov—and other credit resources that may add more confusion and frustration than lasting results, or you can choose to know and use "Remember **NUTTI or MUTTI** in your GUTTI to improve your credit score forevermore"—and use the knowledge that you have gained in a manner where you will apply what you have learned to manage and improve your credit in a more stress-free, effective, efficient and results oriented manner!

You must always remember that your worthiness, character, capacity, and general reputation plays a major factor in your credit score. It is important that you choose to **"properly focus"** and leave excuses behind—and by comprehending and applying "Remember **NUTTI or MUTTI** in your GUTTI to improve your credit score forevermore" on a consistent basis you can put yourself in position to manage your credit effectively for years to come.

You also should know that by mastering "Remember **NUTTI or MUTTI** in your GUTTI to improve your credit score forevermore"—that does not preclude you from learning additional credit systems and approaches if you have a desire to do so.

However, you must realize that it is truly not necessary for your and your family's future success if you operate in a proactive (gain the knowledge that you need NOW—by using the above acronym in a way that is most beneficial to your credit usage or anticipated credit usage) manner!

It is important that you realize that the amount of credit that is made available to you is often based on the income that you earn in your household and other factors.

It is also important that you realize that your failure to understand how to manage your credit and finances is your choice and you must further realize that you are responsible for not only your future success, but the success of your family and other loved ones as well!

If you have an established and functional **(mental working knowledge)** system of attacking your credit and finances, you can more precisely and more accurately determine what lies ahead (plan better) for you and your family in the financial realm of your and your family's life!

You must live your life purposely and with a real willingness to achieve what you desire!

A **comprehensive system of approaching your credit and finances** leaves nothing to chance—and is an approach that those who truly desire success utilize on a consistent basis!

3)

The final structuring technique in the **"3 Step Approach"** that can help you improve your finances is listed below.

My EYES TEAR

- My eyes tear when I see that my financial picture is clear.
- My eyes tear when I see that my financial independence is near.
- My eyes tear when all my credit card balances disappear.

- My eyes tear when I realize I have no financial fear.
- My eyes tear when I know that I have succeeded this year.

If you were to look at the above poem on the surface it would have some meaning to you. However, the real power of the poem lies beneath the surface—and when properly applied could easily change your mindset or the way that you look at finance in general.

Acronyms can play a key role in simplifying complex problems and can make the mind work easier and eliminate or reduce your stress levels.

In the above poem your **eyes** are your (**ii's**) and your **tears** are your (**teeer**). Let me explain further so that you have a clear understanding.

The above poem is a "play on words." In your financial life you should be concerned with your **i**nsurance and **i**nvestments or another way of looking at it, your **eyes** (**ii**).

In your financial life you should also be concerned with your **t**axes, **e**mergency fund,

education planning, **e**state planning/wills, and **r**etirement planning or another way of looking at it, your **tear** (**teeer**).

- By simply remembering the poem above or simply the title of the poem—you bring clarity to your financial understanding immediately.

- By reciting the poem or a line in the poem **daily, weekly, monthly or whatever time frame you prefer** you get to a point where you know <u>all of the areas of your finances that you need to address immediately</u>—thus reducing your stress level or unhealthy concern about your finances.

- Used in conjunction with **BIB N**, Remember **NUTTI or MUTTI** in my GUTTI to improve my credit score forevermore—**my eyes tear** when I see that my financial picture is clear has the real effect of **"you knowing all of the areas of your finances that you must address"** at the drop of a hat.

- This alone would greatly reduce the stress in your life and give you a feeling of well-being in your financial realm for the rest of your life—**particularly after you address and improve each area to the maximum effect possible based on your financial condition**—and you can address those areas more appropriately at this time by going to www.realty-1-strategic-advisors.com—NOW—and/or purchasing **Managing & Improving your Credit & Finances for this MILLENNIUM**!

- Although what you have just learned are simple concepts—by reciting and understanding the concepts behind what the acronyms stand for, you have immediately brought clarity to your credit and financial life and that alone would put you well ahead of the general population as far as understanding your credit and finances.

- You have just had the opportunity to master these life-changing acronyms, keep them in the forefront of your mind as you go through life—as by doing so you will improve your and your family's credit and financial future well-being—quite significantly!

Can you believe that a **"3 Step Approach"** that utilizes **7 words**—has provided the mental framework that allows you to know in a **comprehensive manner what you need to do for the rest of your life** to manage your credit and finances in a highly effective and efficient manner?

However, don't take the above statement at face value! You must seriously ask yourself—do I have a system that does the above, or do I know of a system that does?

BONUS SECTION: Investment Simplification & Wealth Building

Learn how you can at this time choose the right investment vehicle(s) to effectively reach your investment goals...

It is important that you start your long-term investing at the earliest time possible and there are investment vehicles that you can utilize to get you where you need to be more efficiently.

In this bonus section you will learn some of the most useful and time-tested investment vehicles that you can use to build wealth and reach goals that you desire at the various stages of your life.

Your path to **investment success** does not have to be a difficult one if you start early, invest consistently and you know your "target number" that you need to reach to fulfill your various goals.

Your home purchase, college funding, traveling around the world, reaching your retirement number or reaching the number that you need to reach for any other purpose is attainable if you are at this time willing to make a serious effort toward achieving what you desire.

Mutual Funds (MFs)

A **Mutual fund** is an investment program funded by shareholders that trades in diversified holdings and is professionally managed. It normally includes a "bundle of stocks" and investment products and frees you from the hassle of selecting individual stocks or other investments yourself.

A **MF** is a portfolio of stocks, bonds and other securities and creates a diversified investment portfolio that generally reduces your risk factor. It is key that you understand that mutual funds are **"bought and sold"** at the **"end of"** the trading day!

- Mutual funds are sold based on dollars, so **"you can specify any dollar amount"** that you'd like to invest.

- Mutual funds are divided into several kinds of categories, representing the kinds of securities they invest in, their investment objectives, and the type of returns they seek. Although there are others, most mutual funds fall into categories which include **stock** funds, **money market** funds, **bond** funds, and **target-date** funds.

- Mutual funds charge annual fees, expense ratios, or commissions, which may affect their overall returns and you want to ensure that the fund that you select has reasonable fees.

- Employer-sponsored retirement plans commonly invest in mutual funds and if your employer offers them—especially with an employee match, you want to put yourself in position to contribute as best you can, based on your financial ability to do so.

Index Funds (IFs)

Technically a Mutual Fund, **Index funds** invest in stocks that correspond with a major market index such as the S&P 500, Nasdaq or the Dow Jones Industrial Average (DJIA). It could be one focused on a sector, such as healthcare, durable goods or technology. This investment strategy requires less research from analysts and advisors, so your expenses as a shareholder would be lower, and these funds are often designed with **cost-sensitive** investors in mind.

- The positives of index funds are that they require little financial knowledge, are low cost, and are convenient to invest in. On the negative side, you could end up stuck with poorly performing assets and the potential for returns to be less than those of successful managers of actively managed funds.

- The goal of index fund managers are to mirror the performance of a particular index – and not try to outperform it, which is the goal of managers of active funds.

- Although many think that index funds are relatively new, the first publicly available index fund was launched back in the mid-1970s.

- Index funds **often perform better than actively managed funds over longer** investment time frames. Even so, there are still risks involved with this style of investing. If the tracked index falls, then your investment's value will follow and if it is at the time of your retirement or planned withdrawal, you will suffer financially, and your living conditions could be affected.

- You can reduce risk by diversifying your portfolio by holding several different index funds covering a variety of stock markets or sectors.

- Index funds can provide a very straightforward, cost-effective, and diversified way for you to steadily increase your wealth over time. Fund managers do not decide which individual investments they should buy or sell, which is what happens in active mutual funds.

- *Investors in these products expect their chosen index to rise over the long term, even if it encounters some turbulence along the way! The performance of the FTSE All-World Index, which has delivered an average annual return of 9.3% since 1993, according to Vanguard, provides a real world blueprint (30 plus years of results) of what index funds can achieve **IF** utilized appropriately.*

- So, should you choose as a novice investor an active mutual fund(s) or index fund(s)? You can spread your risk by investing a portion in each at the level that you are comfortable with. Again, index funds replicate the performance of an index, whereas the managers of mutual funds will pick and choose securities they believe will help them outperform that index.

- Even though there is more risk, if an active manager makes the right calls, then they can substantially outperform their benchmark index and deliver better returns.

Popular index funds that you may want to consider include the following:

*Fidelity 500 Index Fund (FXAIX)

*Schwab S & P 500 Index Fund (SWPPX)

*T. Rowe Price Equity Index 500 Fund (PREIX)

*Vanguard 500 Index Fund Investor Shares (VFINX)

*Many others

Be sure to do your own independent research, confirm that fees are low, and you can do so by going directly to the sites by "typing in the ticker symbol" using your favorite search engine!

Target Date Funds (TDFs)

Although technically a mutual fund, **target date funds** are separated out in this bonus section in order to give you more clarity on how you can use them to build wealth.

Target-date funds are a "set it and forget it" or "invest it and rest" retirement savings option that removes two headaches for you as an investor:

1) deciding on a mix of assets which saves you time and

2) re-balancing your investments for you over time which saves you time

Target-date funds, also known as **life-cycle funds** or **target-retirement funds**—aim to continually strike the right balance between the risk necessary to build wealth and safer options to protect a growing nest egg.

The fund automatically re-balances your portfolio with the right mix of stocks, bonds and money market accounts as you age and is a great hands-off way for you to build wealth if that fits your personality and risk profile!

Target Date Funds are "mutual funds" that **purchase from other mutual funds** (known in the "investment world" as a "fund of funds") and they are designed to build a diverse portfolio. While you set and forget or invest and rest so to speak, the fund updates your asset allocation over the years for you.

Early in your working life, a target-date fund generally is set for growth by having a much larger slice of your portfolio in stocks rather than fixed-income investments like bonds, which are safer but provide smaller returns (the approach is similar to that of a 529 education savings plan). As your retirement year approaches, the fund gradually shifts toward more bonds, money market accounts and other lower-risk investments.

Your retirement year is the "target date" of most of these funds—unless you choose a target date for other purposes, and the funds are conveniently named to correspond with your planned retirement year. Say you are 35 years old and plan to work until you are 65, a Target Date 2055 would possibly be of appeal to you. Most target-date funds are named in **five-year increments with some at 10-year**

increments, so you would choose the provider with a fund named with the year nearest your planned retirement date or other target date based on your goals.

Below you will find some of the more popular target date funds that you may want to consider:

Vanguard Target 2045 Fund Investor Shares VTIVX

Fidelity Freedom Index 2045 Fund Investor Class FIOFX

Lifecycle Index 2045 Fund Premier Class TLMPX

American Funds 2045 Target Date Retirement Fund Class R-5 REHTX

T Rowe Price Retirement 2045 Fund TRRKX

There are many other target date funds, and the current data is current as of market close on February 1, 2024. Be sure to do your own independent research as the accuracy of the data cannot be guaranteed.

Always realize that the main appeal of target-date funds for most is their simplicity. And just as an index fund operates with simplicity, so too does a target date fund!

The funds go from a "high ratio" of riskier equity funds to safer investments like bonds, and money market accounts as they get closer to the "target date", **freezing your asset allocation** to protect your nest egg.

An important question to ask yourself or your advisor when choosing among target-date funds is whether the account will freeze the year you plan to retire, or whether a “through” fund that continues the glide path for 5, 10, 15, or 20 years past retirement before freezing your asset allocation will be in effect. You want to plan your approach appropriately and select the fund that's right for your retirement or other goals.

How to purchase:

*through your retirement plan

*directly from fund

*open brokerage account ($500 to $3,000 to open)

Exchange Traded Funds (ETFs)

They are similar to **Mutual Funds** as just a few key differences set them apart. The biggest similarity between **ETFs (**Exchange-**T**raded **F**unds) and mutual funds are that they both represent professionally managed collections **(or "baskets")** of individual stocks, bonds or other investments.

However, investment minimums are normally lower with an ETF! You can purchase an ETF share of ***Vanguard FTSE Emerging Markets*** *for under $100. Many more ETF shares start at $500 or more, and you can learn more about ETF offerings by visiting VettaFi financial website.*

- It is key that you understand that **ETFs** allow you to trade **"throughout the trading day"** at market prices. This flexibility **is a key difference** in how the **fund** works as compared to a mutual fund. This level of flexibility may be utilized by active traders making moves throughout the day.

- The main difference between ETFs and mutual funds are that an ETFs price is based on the market price and is sold only in **"full"** shares. Mutual funds, however, are sold based on dollars, so **"you can specify any dollar amount"** that you'd like to invest.

- As an investor, **you have options** and can reap the benefits of diversification.

CALCULATORS Visit: TheWealthIncreaser.com

When you are investing you must know that your goals, risk-tolerance, income and your personal situation must also be taken into serious consideration.

If you currently owe $100,000 on your home mortgage and you desire to pay it off in 5 years, you will need to do some analysis and not just choose the first thing that comes to your mind. If your monthly payment is $1,000 and $500 of your mortgage payment is going toward principal, in 5 years your balance would be roughly $70,000 if you continued on that path.

By adding $1,200 to the monthly payment of $1,000 you could pay $2,200 monthly ($1,700 going toward your principal) and have your mortgage paid off in 5 years, however you would be responsible for paying your property taxes (mandatory) and insurance (optional after your home is paid off, but generally makes sense to have).

Or you could choose an investment strategy of investing the $1,200 per month for 5 years in the market and based on historical trends you could have over $90,000 after 5 years, and since you continued your mortgage payments at $500 per month in principal payments, you would owe $70,000 and therefore have an addition $20,000 plus after the payoff of your mortgage, in your pocket by doing so--assuming your returns were as expected.

In this example inflation is assumed to be 3% and your rate of return is assumed to be 9%. Even if you only assumed a rate of return of 3% (same as inflation) you would have over $80,000, which would still put you ahead by over $10,000 after the payoff of your mortgage. As long as you have a positive return you will come out ahead based on the assumptions mentioned above.

If after 5 years of investing you had a negative return you would possibly fall short of the $70,000 that was needed and you could decide to ride the market longer and pay off the mortgage later, cash in, in spite of the losses and payoff as much as you could on the mortgage.

As you can see from this example, your goals, risk tolerance, income and personal situation will play a large part in ***how you decide to pay off your debt*** *and how you select your investments!*

You want to know how to invest properly on the front end and you want to know that you can **invest inside of your retirement account(s)** (your earnings will grow tax free) and avoid taxes for years or **outside of your retirement account(s)** (you will provide 1099 and other paperwork to your tax professional that your brokerage would send to you at tax time) where you would possibly owe taxes on an annual basis (ETFs and Index funds are often tax efficient even outside of retirement accounts).

If you are age 25 and desire to **retire by age 55** with your house paid off and **over 4 million** in your account in today's dollars, you would have to invest $1,600 monthly for 30 years assuming 3% inflation and a 10% rate of return—and also assuming you pay your house off within that 30-year period.

Therefore, in the above examples, your returns would be affected depending on the type of investment and whether the investment is inside or outside of your retirement accounts. Once you reach age 59 1/2 you can withdraw your retirement funds without incurring an early withdrawal penalty, however you would pay taxes at your ordinary income rate, unless the distributions were from a ROTH IRA or there was an exception that applied.

Mandatory withdrawals from your traditional IRA or retirement plan would be required once you reached age 73, however with a ROTH IRA, there are no mandatory withdrawals, however after your death your beneficiaries must take required minimum distributions!

Also realize that you can choose **balanced funds** that invest in a hybrid of asset classes, whether stocks, bonds, money market instruments, or alternative investments. The objective of this fund, known as an asset allocation fund, is to reduce the risk of exposure across asset classes.

In closing, it is important that you realize that this discussion is not about theory or what you possibly need to do, but what you **CAN** do! You must at this time analyze your income and expenses and determine your discretionary income that you have available so that you can start investing now, get more income by creating a plan to increase your income whether by the payoff of your debt, scaling back on your entertainment and other expenses, or finding other ways to get income on a consistent basis.

Although you will hear many financial planners tout the fact that you can increase your savings and come up with a significant amount to invest by scaling back on the $5 that you spend daily on your favorite latte or coffee, that is not something that we are a big proponent of as we realize that for some, a $5 cup of coffee can give them the added energy that is needed to help them earn more on a daily, weekly and annual basis, therefore they more than offset the $100 or so that they spend on a monthly basis on coffee that they could be using for investing.

However there are other ways that you can get more income and cut expenses and you may want to analyze and pursue them!

Once you determine the amount of income that you have available to invest and you commit to investing that or another amount over a "period of time" **you can start on a path to reaching the number that you need to attain your goal(s)** and live daily with more joy on the inside!

Whether your discretionary or available funds to invest are $200 per month or $2,000 per month and you decide to use it to invest long-term, you can achieve significant results over a 30-year period. By calculating what you can do now, **(you need to know your discretionary or available income that you have to invest, whether you will invest weekly, monthly, yearly or a one-time lump-sum investment and furthermore you need to know the "time frame that is needed or desired" to reach your goal)** you can determine the nest egg that you can have by investing consistently in a relatively painless way—starting today.

Investing $200 monthly at 3% inflation and a 9% rate of return will give you over $500,000 (five-hundred thousand) in 30 years!

The 4 percent raise that you get, the promotion that you get, or working one or two days a month for lyft, uber, grubhub or other "new economy" options can easily provide you that cushion to invest either temporarily or permanently over the next 30 years.

In many cases, you can find $200 by analyzing your monthly spending and tightening up your budget some. You can do a detailed analysis of your insurance products, taxes and other areas of your finances and discover new savings or increases in income. The ways that you can come up with the needed funds for long-term wealth building success is endless, if you want to achieve your goals in a sincere manner!

Investing $2,000 monthly at 3% inflation and a 9% rate of return will give you over $5,000,000 (five million) in 30 years!

To get that extra $2,000 per month, you may have to start a business, have your stay-at-home spouse find employment either part-time or full-time, or determine other ways to increase your monthly income based on your creativity and the unique skills that you now have or will cultivate in the near future.

In many instances high net worth and high-income earners wasted hundreds if not thousands on a monthly basis on frivolous or unnecessary spending that could be utilized more appropriately for building long-term wealth of significant amounts.

What is the **discretionary amount** that you "need or want to get to" so that you can invest at this time and in your future, to work towards making life more manageable for you and your loved ones?

How You Can Invest using Mutual Funds, Index Funds, Target Date Funds and Exchange-Traded-Funds:

1. Make sure you have a brokerage account with enough cash on hand, and with access to mutual fund shares and other investments.
2. Identify specific mutual funds or ETFs that match your investing goals in terms of risk, returns, fees, and minimum investments. Some brokerage platforms offer fund screening and research tools.
3. Determine how much you want to invest initially and submit your trade. If you choose, you can set up automatic recurring investments in the amount that you desire.
4. Monitor and review performances periodically, making adjustments as needed.
5. When it is time to close your position, enter a sell order on your platform.
6. Realize that with some funds you can invest directly and depending on the fund type, the functions mentioned above will be done by the fund manager or brokerage.

While many mutual funds are no-load, you can often avoid brokerage fees and commissions by purchasing a fund directly from the mutual fund company instead of going through an intermediary or third party.

There are pros and cons of investing utilizing mutual funds and you can go to investopedia.com to learn more about investing in a simplified, yet effective manner!

Some funds are defined with a specific allocation strategy that is fixed, so the investor can have a predictable exposure to various asset classes. Other funds follow a strategy for dynamic allocation percentages to meet various investor objectives. This may include responding to market conditions, business cycle changes, or the changing phases of the investor's own life.

The portfolio manager is commonly given the freedom to switch the ratio of asset classes as needed to maintain the integrity of the fund's stated strategy.

Below you will find what is often included in mutual funds, including balanced funds, index funds, target date funds, and exchange-traded funds.

Money Market Funds

The money market consists of safe, risk-free, short-term debt instruments, mostly government Treasury bills. An investor will not earn substantial returns, but the principal is guaranteed. A typical return is a little more than the amount earned in a regular checking or savings account and a little less than the average certificate of deposit (CD).

Income Funds

Income funds are named for their purpose: to provide current income on a steady basis. These funds invest primarily in government and high-quality corporate debt, holding these bonds until maturity to provide interest streams. While fund holdings may appreciate, the primary objective of these funds are to provide steady cash flow to investors. As such, the audience for these funds consists of conservative investors and retirees.

International/Global Funds

An international fund, or foreign fund, invests only in assets located outside an investor's home country. Global funds, however, can invest anywhere around the world. Their volatility often depends on the unique country's economy and political risks. However, these funds can be part of a well-balanced portfolio by increasing diversification, since the returns in foreign countries may be uncorrelated with returns at home.

Specialty Funds

Sector funds are targeted strategy funds aimed at specific sectors of the economy, such as financial, technology, or health care. Sector funds can be extremely volatile since the stocks in a given sector tend to be highly correlated with each other.

Regional funds make it easier to focus on a specific geographic area of the world. This can mean focusing on a broader region or an individual country.

Socially responsible funds, or ethical funds, invest only in companies that meet the criteria of certain guidelines or beliefs. For example, some socially responsible funds do not invest in "sin" industries such as tobacco, alcoholic beverages, weapons, or nuclear power. Other funds invest primarily in green technology, such as solar and wind power or recycling. Fidelity Charitable and other "Socially Responsible Investment Funds" are now available in abundance in the investment world.

Other

Bond, precious metals, natural resources, crypto and other investment products are now packaged and sold as mutual funds in some instances.

You can **use the above approaches** to ensure you reach your "retirement number" or "other goals" that you have—and use other riskier or more aggressive approaches to further build wealth if you are in position to do so.

Investing a **percentage of** your investments in mutual funds, index funds, target date funds and ETF funds can be a painless and simple way for you to build wealth and live out your retirement with dignity. Automatic Investing (dollar-cost averaging) $200 monthly in a mutual fund, $200 monthly in an index fund, $200 monthly in a target date fund and $200 monthly in an ETF fund **(total of $800 monthly)** will provide you with a hefty return over time, if market trends continue. You can also invest $200 per week and invest automatically if you feel that will work better for you.

The above approaches, along with your social security, pension, and possibly other retirement income can put you well ahead of most, if you start early and invest consistently. You no longer must fake it until you make it, you can now be true to yourself as you are now on a serious path toward making your dreams come true, because you decided to take your mind off the shelf!

Isn't it time that you use a "more pragmatic approach" toward investing and building wealth?

Always realize that you have **numerous options** to choose from in the investment world regardless of your goals, however the process of **investing in an effective manner is not that complicated**, unless you make it complicated. In this short (relative to what you have learned) **bonus section**, you have learned how you can invest in a straightforward manner and achieve realistic results that can enhance your living conditions while you are here on planet earth.

All the best to your tax, investment, and wealth building success...

Publisher: TFA Financial Planning

Email: tj@TheWealthIncreaser.com

Thomas (TJ) Underwood is the CEO of TFA Financial Planning—one of the most successful tax and financial planning companies in the metropolitan Atlanta area. TFA Financial Planning is based out of Atlanta, GA.

He is a former fee-only financial planner and top producing loan processor, and he has assisted clients from as far away as Germany with their financial concerns. The concepts in "Taxing Subject Matters Made Easy" have been utilized by savvy taxpayers to help them build wealth and achieve many of their major tax and financial goals.

The concepts in this beginners' guide are designed to enhance successful outcomes for those who pay income and other taxes in the United States and is a valuable addition to all households who desire to maximize their tax knowledge and build wealth more efficiently.

He is also the creator of TheWealthIncreaser.com, one of the leading financial blog sites that can be found in the internet universe.

Taxing Subject Matters Made Easy

Taxing Subject Matters Created for Your Wealth Building Success

ISBN: 978-1-953994-24-0

Publisher: TFA Financial Planning

Email: tj@TheWealthIncreaser.com

Afterword

Since the completion of **Taxing Subject Matters Made Easy** in the spring of 2025, major changes have occurred as a result of the so called "**B**ig, **B**eautiful, **B**ill" that passed the house and senate in July and was signed into law on July 4th of 2025.

As the author of **Taxing Subject Matters Made Easy,** I found it imperative to include an update of the major changes that occurred because of the so called "BBB" that is now law in the United States tax system.

As a result of the new so called **B**ig **B**eautiful **B**ill federal estate taxes and other changes that occurred receive some clarification as of July 4th, 2025, with some of the key changes being presented in this Afterword!

Keep in mind the detailed analysis of the new bill is yet to be interpreted by the IRS, however key points that you must be aware of because of the bill include the **new estate tax exemption amounts** are now 13.99 million for tax year 2025 and adjusted for inflation for the years after 2025.

In addition to understanding the "federal estate tax rates" and when you could potentially be liable to pay, you also want to be aware of **either state estate tax rates** or **state inheritance tax rates** as they can both further reduce the amount of proceeds you will receive or increase the amount of tax that you must pay.

Other key changes include the following:

2025 Tax & Spending Bill Tax Highlights

- Above line $1,000 ($2,000 MFJ) charitable cash contribution now available, meaning that even if you don't itemize you can take the deduction if you qualify.

- Below the line SALT (State And Local Tax) deduction increases to $40,000 (you must itemize to claim) for 2025 and the cap increases by 1 percent from that **level through 2029**, subject to a phaseout for taxpayers with incomes above $500,000, then the cap reduces to a **flat $10,000** thereafter (after 2029).

- Dependent Credit still $500.

- Overtime deduction or exclusion now available for those who qualify. **$12,500 ($25,000 for joint filers) of the premium portion of overtime compensation is now deductible for itemizers and non-itemizers for tax years 2025 through 2028**; the deduction phases out at a 10 percent rate when adjusted gross income exceeds $150,000 ($300,000 for joint filers).

- No tax on tips included in bill for those who qualify. Up to $25,000 of **tip income may be** deductible for individuals in traditionally and customarily tipped industries **for tax years 2025 through 2028**; deduction phases out at a 10 percent rate when adjusted gross income exceeds $150,000 ($300,000 for joint filers).

- Possible Social Security tax reduction for those who qualify.

- Medicare work requirements go into effect in **December 2026**, Hospital and Health care issues are a concern of many due to the Medicare provisions in the bill.

- Tax rate filing requirements for 2025 tax year are now: $31,500 for joint filers, $23,625 for head of household, and $15,750 for all other filers, inflation adjusted thereafter.

- Made the personal exemption elimination permanent.
- Temporarily added a senior deduction of $6,000 for each qualifying individual for both itemizers and non-itemizers that phases out when modified adjusted gross income exceeds $75,000, available from 2025 through 2028.
- Made the expiring **child** tax credit **permanent** with an increased maximum of $2,200 in 2026, inflation adjusted thereafter.
- Made the $750,000 principal limit for the home mortgage interest deduction permanent.
- Made other changes and limitations to itemized deduction permanent, including the limitation on personal casualty losses, **termination of the miscellaneous itemized deduction** (except for educator expenses), Pease limitation on itemized deductions, and certain moving expenses (except for active-duty members of the armed forces and members of the intelligence community).
- Limited the value of itemized deductions to 35 cents on the dollar for taxpayers in the top tax bracket.
- Made the increase in the alternative minimum tax (AMT) exemption permanent; revert AMT exemption phaseout thresholds to 2018 levels of $500,000 for single filers and $1 million for joint returns, indexed for inflation thereafter; increased the phaseout rate. NIIT still in effect.
- Created a 0.5 percent floor on itemized deductions for charitable contributions.
- Repealed several **Inflation Reduction Act** green energy tax credits primarily aimed at individuals, such as **electric**

vehicle and residential energy efficiency credits, either after 2025 or within a year of the law's enactment.

- **Temporarily made auto loan interest deductible for itemizers and non-itemizers for new autos with final assembly in the United States for tax years 2025 through 2028**; deduction limited to $10,000 and phases out at a 20 percent rate when income exceeds $100,000 for single filers and $200,000 for joint filers.

- Qualified Business Income **(QBI)** deduction was increased from **20□percent to 23□percent** for pass-through entities. Rooted in Section□199A of the tax code, this deduction is now permanent, replacing the fading expiration of 2025—and it provides small business owners and potential small business owners the ability to approach taxes, planning, and reinvestment in a more favorable manner.

- **Reporting Threshold for 3rd Party Apps Increased**

  Before the BBB, third-party apps had to report over $600 in payments per year to the IRS. This rule caused confusion and unexpected tax paperwork among casual sellers and entrepreneurs who were just starting out.

Now, the bill has changed the reporting limits; third-party apps are only required to send Form 1099-K if you have over $20,000 in payments and over 200 transactions in a calendar year. Although you're still required to report any business income you receive through these platforms on your taxes, this change reduces the reporting burden for both sellers and the IRS.

- **Estate taxes exemption amount clarified**

Even if you avoid the federal estate tax (13.99 million for tax year 2025) you may very well be liable at the state level, depending on where you reside. The states that levy an ***estate tax*** *or* ***inheritance tax*** *include the following:*

These states levy an estate tax:

- Connecticut
- Washington
- Hawaii
- Illinois
- Maine
- **Maryland**
- Massachusetts
- New York
- Oregon
- Rhode Island
- Vermont
- Washington, D.C.

What is the inheritance tax?

Unlike an estate tax, which is **paid by the estate "before" the assets are distributed**, an inheritance tax is **paid by the beneficiary** on the assets' value.

The tax is levied if the person who died lived in a state that has an inheritance tax, even if the beneficiary lives in a state without an inheritance tax!

The inheritance tax rate, as well as which assets it applies to, and which beneficiaries must pay it, varies by state. Each state has its own rules (more on that later).

How inheritance tax works

In states with an inheritance tax (see list below to see if the state that you or your loved ones reside in is listed), **beneficiaries pay** a tax on the value of their inheritance. Often, the inheritance tax is a progressive tax, which means the tax rate increases with the value of the bequest. A progressive tax system employs a series of tax rates, whereas a flat tax system generally uses one tax rate for all income levels.

Some states assess different tax rates depending on the asset received, or the beneficiary's relationship to the person who died. Close relatives may be exempt from the inheritance tax or may pay a lower rate.

In 2024, the *highest* **inheritance tax** rate among the **five states** (remember, states usually levy a range of inheritance tax rates) ranged from 10 to 16 percent, with New Jersey and Kentucky having the highest top rate of 16 percent.

Always realize that state laws vary and are subject to change!

Some states, including Nebraska, New Jersey and Maryland offer an **inheritance tax exemption**, which allows the beneficiary to avoid the inheritance tax if the asset's value is less than the exemption amount.

For example, in Nebraska, immediate relatives are given a $100,000 exemption— close relatives pay a 1 percent tax on the value of inherited assets exceeding $100,000.

In New Jersey, spouses, domestic partners, children and grandchildren are exempt from paying inheritance taxes.

Some beneficiaries, including siblings of the person who died, pay inheritance tax rates of 11 to 16 percent after a $25,000 exemption.

Other beneficiaries, including aunts, uncles and cousins, pay rates of 11 to 16 percent on the entire inheritance, without the benefit of an exemption amount.

Maryland offers an inheritance tax exemption for property worth less than $1,000; the state also exempts surviving spouses, children, grandchildren, great-grandchildren, parents and grandparents from paying an inheritance tax.

These are the states that levy an inheritance tax:

While the "decedent is responsible" (by reading this book that is not you) for **estate taxes**, the beneficiaries (could be you) must pay the inheritance tax!

You would pay an estate tax at the federal level if applicable, and if you lived in a state with an estate tax ***or*** *inheritance tax and you were the beneficiary and was not otherwise exempt you would have an additional tax.*

So, if you receive property if someone passes and assets were left for you, you might be liable to pay estate tax at the *federal level* and/or *estate* **or** *inheritance tax* at the state level.

Only certain states use the inheritance tax, **instead of** the estate tax and they include:

- Iowa
- Kentucky

- **Maryland**
- Nebraska
- New Jersey
- Pennsylvania

Maryland is the only state with both an estate tax and an inheritance tax! And as of 2025 Iowa will phase out its inheritance tax!

Also, it doesn't matter if you live outside of those states that have an inheritance tax. If you inherit from someone who lived in Nebraska, but you live in Arkansas, you might still owe money to Nebraska.

The amount beneficiaries pay because of the tax varies. This is because the amount you pay can depend not only on "how much you receive" but also on "your relationship" with the deceased.

Certain exceptions or exemptions may apply to allow you to receive assets without paying an inheritance tax on them.

For example, Maryland does not place an inheritance tax on property passed on to a surviving spouse or direct descendants. Alternatively, New Jersey doesn't tax assets left to children or a surviving spouse, but the decedent's siblings "are" liable.

Each state has its own base threshold and marginal rate. So, if you live in any of the states above, it's best to research the rules proactively so you know what responsibilities you have if it is your loved one, someone you know or even if it was you who transitioned and left assets behind!

A key point to remember is that an inheritance tax is **levied when a beneficiary inherits assets** from the estate of someone who died, in five states in the United States that were listed above.

However, you are not in the clear if you don't live in one of the five states as **12 states** have an "estate tax" that the estate would pay (not you) so you want to know your responsibilities in those states as well.

*Again, there is no federal inheritance tax, but **five states** currently levy state inheritance tax: Kentucky, **Maryland**, Nebraska, New Jersey and Pennsylvania. (Iowa was a sixth state on that list until it ended its inheritance tax starting in 2025).*

> *There **is** federal estate tax, and **twelve states** currently levy a state estate tax: Connecticut, Washington, Hawaii, Illinois, Maine, **Maryland**, Massachusetts, New York, Oregon, Rhode Island, Vermont, and Washington, D.C. (technically not a state). Gift tax rules were not changed in the BBB!*

To reiterate, the federal government **does** levy an estate tax, as do 12 states and Washington, D.C. mentioned above. Maryland is highlighted above because it assesses **both** an estate tax and an inheritance tax.

Other Business Tax Provisions of BBB

- Permanently restore immediate expensing for domestic research and development (R&D) expenses; small businesses with gross receipts of $31 million or less can retroactively expense R&D back to after 12/31/21; all other domestic R&D between 12/21/21 and 1/1/25 can accelerate remaining deductions over a one- or two-year period.
- Permanently reinstate the EBITDA-based limitation on business net interest deductions.
- Permanently restore 100 percent bonus depreciation for short-lived investments.

- Temporarily provide 100 percent expensing of qualifying structures, with the beginning of construction occurring after Jan. 19, 2025, and before Jan. 19, 2029, and placed in service before Jan. 1, 2031.
- Made the Section 199A pass-through deduction permanent; increase phase-in range of limitation by $50,000 for non-joint returns and $100,000 for joint returns; create a minimum deduction of $400 for taxpayers with $1,000 or more of qualified business income (QBI) for material participants.
- Implement a 1 percent floor on deduction of charitable contributions made by corporations.
- Eliminate clean electricity production credit (45Y) and investment credit (48E) for projects placed in service after 2027, except for projects that begin construction within 12 months of passage and baseload power sources such as nuclear, hydropower, geothermal, and battery storage; introduce restrictions related to foreign entities of concern (FEOC).
- Extend the clean fuel production credit (45Z) until 2030 and expand eligibility.
- Introduce FEOC restrictions for several other credits, including the nuclear production credit (45U), the clean fuel production credit (45Z), the carbon oxide sequestration credit (45Q), and the advanced manufacturing production credit (45X); alter phaseouts and eligibility for 45X and 45Q.
- Require intangible drilling and development costs to be taken into account for the purposes of computing adjusted financial statement income.
- Add income from hydrogen storage, carbon capture, advanced nuclear, hydropower, and geothermal energy to

qualifying income of certain publicly traded partnerships treated as C corporations.

International Tax Provisions of BBB

- Rename GILTI to Net CFC Tested Income (NCTI) and establish a 12.6 percent to 14 percent top rate after foreign tax credit treatment. Eliminate indirect expense allocation, raise foreign tax creditability to 90 percent, and remove the QBAI (qualified business asset investment) exclusion for the deemed return on physical capital. Also includes some miscellaneous base broadeners.
- Rename FDII to Foreign-Derived Deduction Eligible Income (FDDEI), and establish a 14 percent rate, with parallel changes to those in GILTI.
- Raise the BEAT rate to 10.5 percent and preserve current policy on allowability of US tax credits under BEAT.

Other Provisions were included in the bill that are too numerous to discuss at this time, however the highlights of the bill that will affect many have been outlined above.

Some other provisions (some repeated due to their importance) that may be of concern to many include:

- QOF (Qualified Opportunity Zone Fund) made permanent: No longer will investors face the uncertainty of potential program expiration, enabling longer-term planning and more substantial commitments to community development projects. This stability should prove particularly attractive to institutional investors who have historically been cautious about programs with sunset clauses. Under this new framework, investors who deploy capital gains into qualified opportunity funds after December 31, 2026, will still enjoy the permanent elimination of capital gains taxes on their opportunity zone investments held for at least 10 years—the program's signature benefit remains intact.

The new system offers **a rolling five-year deferral period** for the initial capital gains invested, replacing the current program's more complex timeline that provided basis step-ups at five and seven years before the final tax elimination benefit.

The legislation introduces a tiered approach to basis step-ups, acknowledging the varying challenges of different investment environments. Standard QOF investors will receive a **10% basis step-up after five years**, providing modest tax relief on their original deferred gains.

More significantly, the **bill establishes a new category of qualified rural opportunity funds**, recognizing that rural areas face unique economic challenges that warrant enhanced incentives.

Rural investors will enjoy a 30% basis step-up, a substantial improvement that reflects the higher risks and longer development timelines typically associated with rural investments.

These areas, defined as locations outside cities or towns of 50,000 people or contiguous urbanized areas, will also benefit from a reduced substantial-improvement threshold of 50% rather than the standard 100% requirement.

The enhanced rural incentives create particularly compelling opportunities in the oil and gas sector, where many projects are naturally located in rural areas that could qualify for qualified rural opportunity fund status.

The 30% basis step-up, combined with the reduced improvement threshold and ultimate tax-free treatment of gains, **could potentially make rural energy projects among the most tax-efficient investments available to investors** seeking both energy sector exposure and community development impact.

One of the most consequential aspects of the Big Beautiful Bill involves the periodic redesignation of opportunity zones themselves.

Starting July 1, 2026, **governors will be required to select new Census tracts every decade**, with the first new designations taking effect January 1, 2027.

This rolling approach ensures that the program's benefits remain targeted toward areas of greatest need rather than becoming entrenched in communities that may have already experienced significant improvement.

The redesignation process will operate under tighter criteria than the original program. The "low-income community" threshold will drop from 80% to 70% of area or statewide median family income.

Additionally, the exception that allowed non-low-income tracts contiguous to qualified areas will disappear, further concentrating benefits in the most economically distressed locations.

Additionally, the **transition period** between the **current program** and **Opportunity Zones 2027** creates a complex strategic landscape for many investors. Those who can deploy capital gains before the December 31, 2026, deadline will enjoy the current program's more generous benefits.

However, a timing quirk in the legislation may discourage some 2026 investments. Investors receiving K-1 distributions or other gains late in 2026 may find themselves better served by waiting until 2027 to make their opportunity zone investments, when they can **take advantage of the new five-year rolling deferral** rather than being locked into the abbreviated timeline of the current program's final year.

Despite the bill's comprehensive nature, several provisions sought by opportunity zone advocates failed to make it into the final legislation.

The QOF program continues to restrict benefits to capital gains, excluding ordinary income and other forms of investment capital!

This limitation has historically made the program less attractive to certain types of investors and may continue to constrain its overall impact.

Affordable housing advocates are disappointed by the absence of additional incentives specifically targeted toward residential development. Given the ongoing affordable housing crisis in many American communities, this omission seems to miss the mark as critical housing needs are in play throughout the United States.

The new tax bill represents both an ending and a beginning for opportunity zone investing. The current program's sunset creates urgency for investors seeking to maximize their tax benefits under existing rules, while the new permanent framework offers long-term stability for community development initiatives.

For you as an investor, the key will be balancing the immediate opportunities available under current rules with the long-term potential of the restructured program. If you are one who can navigate this transition effectively you can find yourself well-positioned to participate in what promises to be a new era of tax-advantaged community development investing using QOF's.

- **The BBB legislation restores tax deductions for mortgage insurance.** MIP/PMI for those who put less than 20% down when they purchase a home using financial products are once again deductible, if you itemize.

- The BBB also expands the low-income housing tax credit for builders who create affordable rental properties.

- The **20% pass-through deduction**, which allows small businesses that are pass-through entities to deduct up to 20% of qualified business income on their federal income tax return was slightly increased, and is now permanent. And starting in 2026, you can get a minimum deduction of $400 if you "materially participate" in a business that earns at least $1,000 in revenue.

- The TCJA **eliminated miscellaneous itemized deductions** and the deduction for **moving expenses** (with a few exceptions) through 2025. The BBB made these changes permanent.

- The $750,000 limit on the **mortgage interest deduction** was made permanent, and **mortgage insurance premiums** can be deducted as part of your mortgage interest **starting in 2026** (returns filed in 2027).

- The Child Tax Credit is worth $2,200 per qualifying child in 2025 and will be adjusted by $100 increments going forward.
  The refundable portion, known as the **Additional Child Tax Credit (ACTC)**, is now $1,700 for the 2025 tax year. The adoption credit will hold steady at $17,280 and is refundable up to $5,000.

- The itemized deduction for personal casualty losses due to a federally declared disaster is now permanent. The bill expanded the provision so it will include certain state-declared disasters starting in 2026.

- **The standard deduction increased**

  You might recall that the standard deduction nearly doubled in 2018 under the TCJA. The Big Beautiful Bill didn't just make this increase permanent—it increased the deduction for 2025. The standard deduction amounts for tax year 2025 are as follows:

Filing Status	Standard Deduction (2025)
Single	$15,750
Married Filing Separately	$15,750
Married Filing Jointly	$31,500
Qualifying Widow(er)	$31,500

Head of Household	$23,625

- **Increased State and Local Tax (SALT) deduction**

When it was signed in 2017, the TCJA put a cap on how much you could deduct for state and local taxes at $10,000. Under the BBB, the limit is temporarily increasing to $40,000 beginning in 2025, and it will increase by 1% for the next five years before it drops back down to $10,000. Here's how this deduction has changed in detail:

Tax Code	SALT Deduction limit	Notes
Before the TCJA (2017 and earlier)	Unlimited	Taxpayers could deduct the full amount of state and local taxes paid
TCJA (2018-2024)	$10,000 ($5,000 if married filing separately)	Limit applied to combined state income, property, and sales taxes
Big Beautiful Bill (2025–2029)	$40,000 ($20,000 if married filing separately)	Limit will increase 1% per year through 2029, then revert to $10,000 in 2030

- **New car loan interest deduction now available**

For 2025 through 2028, up to $10,000 in interest paid on qualifying car loans can be taken as an above-the-line deduction. The vehicle must have been assembled in the U.S., purchased after December 31, 2024, and be for your personal use (not a business vehicle). The deduction **doesn't apply to used or leased vehicles**, and it phases out if your modified AGI is over $100,000 ($200,000 if you file jointly).

- **New deduction for tips and overtime**

  Tips are considered earned income and are still subject to federal income tax withholding, FICA, and Medicare tax. You'll still need to report them on your W-2. But the BBB allows you to deduct up to $25,000 per person in tip income as an above-the-line deduction (no itemizing necessary to qualify).

  If you receive overtime pay, you can deduct the amount you earn above your regular rate (like the "half" in "time-and-a-half") up to $12,500 if you file as single, or $25,000 if you file jointly.

  Both deductions will begin to phase out if your modified AGI as a single filer is $150,000 (or $300,000 for joint filers). These provisions are in effect beginning in 2025 and are set to expire in 2028.

- **Dependent Care FSA limit increase**

  Starting in 2026, the annual contribution limit for **employer-sponsored Dependent Care FSAs** will increase from $5,000 to $7,500 (or from $2,500 to $3,750 if you're married filing separately). This increase means you can set aside more pretax dollars to cover child or dependent care.

- **Child & Dependent Care Credit increased**

In 2026, the Child and Dependent Care Tax Credit will increase to 50% of qualifying care expenses–up to $3,000 for one child or $6,000 for two or more–but it will remain nonrefundable.

- **Changes to the educator expense deduction**

  Beginning in 2026, educator expenses will be claimed as a miscellaneous deduction on Schedule A, **so you'll have to itemize your deductions** to take it. The amount will no longer be capped at $300 per educator. The deduction is expanding to apply to coaches and sports administrators, and the list of qualifying expenses will also include non-instructional athletic equipment.

- **Additional $6,000 deduction for seniors over age 65**

  Taxpayers who are 65 or older already receive an increased standard deduction under the current tax code.

  In 2025, that amount is $2,000 for single filers or heads of household, and $1,600 for those filing jointly ($3,200 if both spouses are age 65).

  With the BBB, **seniors will get a *bonus* deduction of $6,000 per eligible person beginning in 2025** (expiring in 2028).

  This tax break is intended to help offset taxes on Social Security benefits, but you don't have to receive Social Security to qualify.

  This new deduction is an above-the-line deduction, so you can take it whether you itemize your deductions or take the standard deduction.

  The deduction phases out if your modified AGI is more than $75,000 ($150,000 for joint filers).

- **Reduced gambling loss deduction**

  Recall that the TCJA allowed you to deduct 100% of your gambling losses up to the amount you won. This deduction will be reduced starting in 2026, so you can only deduct losses equal to 90% of your winnings.

- **Residential energy and EV credits rolled back**

  The Clean Vehicle Tax Credit will now expire on September 30, 2025, and the Energy Efficient Home Improvement Tax Credit will expire on December 31, 2025. Under the Inflation Reduction Act, these tax incentives weren't set to expire until 2032.

- **Bonus depreciation increased to 100%**

  Businesses can now deduct the full cost of eligible equipment, machinery, and other qualified property in the year it's placed into service, instead of spreading the deduction over time. Bonus depreciation is now permanently set at 100%, instead of 40%.

  The definition of "qualified property" now includes manufacturing buildings—but only if they're placed in service before January 1, 2031. Normally, those buildings would be depreciated slowly over 39 years, so this is a big upfront tax break.

- **Child Tax Credit**

  The BBB ensured that the increase in Child Tax Credit is permanent. Before 2018, the CTC was $1,000 per qualifying child. Under the TCJA and now the BBB, the amount has more than doubled. In 2025, parents can claim **$2,200** per qualifying child.

- **Tax break for overtime**

  Yes, there is now a tax break for overtime if you qualify. Single taxpayers who qualify can claim up to $12,500 of overtime income as an **above-the-line deduction** (up to $25,000 if they're married filing jointly).

- **Are Social Security benefits tax-free now?**

  Possibly for some, but not exactly for others. Social Security income can be taxable, depending on your total income and filing status. The BBB includes a temporary deduction for seniors, but they don't have to receive Social Security to qualify.

- Extension of the cancellation of debt/mortgage forgiveness act was not found in the bill.

- **Home improvement/energy deductions** were significantly modified as key provisions of the Inflation Reduction Act (IRA) are set to sunset early, taxpayers contemplating energy-efficient improvements should consider the new deadlines and take appropriate action:

- Vehicle energy credits set to expire in 2025. With clean vehicle credits (§25E and §30D) **expiring September 30, 2025**, taxpayers considering a clean vehicle purchase should consider **expediting vehicle purchases:** Taxpayers should act quickly to secure clean vehicles before dealer inventory diminishes. Consider pre-ordering to avoid missing deadlines due to supply constraints.

  The Inflation Reduction Act already introduced complexity to energy-related tax credits. Now, the BBB adds more confusion by compressing differing timelines, therefore proactive planning on your part will be necessary!

You should immediately evaluate and execute energy tax credit strategies, ensuring full advantage of remaining federal benefits while at the same time taking a vivid look at your overall finances. Early action and coordinated planning with tax and financial advisors can secure these significant tax incentives before they vanish in 2025. Be sure to combine available credits with local or state incentives where applicable.

- Businesses can now deduct research and development expenses immediately.
- BBB established a 1 percent remittances tax, with many more transactions presumed exempt than under the House version.
- BBB changed the rules for premium tax credits (PTCs), the CTC, and the earned income tax credit (EITC).
- Expanded the **Section 179 expensing cap to an inflation-adjusted $2.5 million** with a phasedown starting when the cost of qualifying property exceeds an inflation-adjusted $4 million; applies after Dec. 31, 2024.
- Raised the tax on student-adjusted endowment of certain private colleges and universities in a new bracketed structure with a top rate of 8 percent, exempting institutions with fewer than 3,000 full-time students.
- Expanded the Section 4960 tax on excess compensation to any employee of an applicable tax-exempt organization that receives remuneration of more than $1 million.

You can learn more about the "BBB" by visiting:

Source: IRS.gov

Source: **H.R.1 - One Big Beautiful Bill Act**

Source: https://taxfoundation.org/research/all/federal/big-beautiful-bill-senate-gop-tax-plan/

Additionally, you want to make the right or better moves because of this legislation and realize that your personal filing status and tax position is unique to you, and you want to timely ensure you know what you need to do to enhance the likelihood of realistically making your dreams come true.

Also realize that the "BBB" cuts the Consumer Financial Protection Bureau's (CFPB) annual funding almost in half—meaning the agency will likely have to carry out the same responsibilities with significantly less money—therefore you as a consumer will have less protection.

That could potentially have a negative effect for consumers for years as scammers and others who prey on the weak and ill-informed will possibly have more room in which to operate.

Even though the BBB has positives and negatives, you want to decipher (or have a competent tax or other professional(s) assist you) what you can take from the bill and plan more effectively for your and your family's future. Always remember that tax planning is a year-round process, and you want to actively participate in your tax and financial success by being involved at some level.

Also, it is important that you realize key components of the bill is what it does not do!

It does not make several provisions in the bill that benefit those with modest income permanent, it does not meaningful reduce the tax burden for those in the lower, middle and upper middle class, it does not protect those on Medicare/Medicaid, but will actually hurt many—and that could lead to difficulty for recipients (and their family) of those services as well as difficulty for health care providers, health insurance companies and those who have private insurance according to many market watchers. It does not restore the employee 2% deduction that has helped many over the years that was available on schedule A!

And in similar fashion as the Tax Cuts and Jobs Act of 2017, the BBB generally does not help those in certain tax brackets permanently reduce their taxes in a meaningful and significant way—therefore uncertainty remains in the atmosphere for many!

Despite what it does not do, you are in position to apply the concepts that you have learned in this book for your greater benefit and you are well on your way to achieving at a high level and building your tax knowledge and income to the level that you desire so that you can live out your life with joy at the center—so that "success" will let you enter—and it is the desire of the author that this book will serve as a powerful mentor.

Even with the changes in the so-called BBB, if you control your actions and apply what you have learned in this book in a manner that can be of benefit to you and your family based on your unique filing status, you can bring success into your household, regardless of this bill or any other tax bill.

However, a key component to your tax and wealth building success is that you must move to action—NOW!

All the best…

Made in the USA
Monee, IL
04 November 2026

67387324R10213